Colin Spencer's

CORDON VERT

A delicious and original dinner party menu for every week of the year, combining the finest seasonal ingredients and complemented with suggestions for the perfect wine, to delight both host and guests alike.

Front cover illustration: Confit Bayeldi (page 149).
Back cover illustration: Salade de Romaine aux Capucines (page 159).

Colin Spencer's

CORDON VERT

52 Vegetarian Gourmet Dinner Party Menus

Illustrated by Paul Davies
Edited by Lee Faber

GUILD PUBLISHING
LONDON

This edition published 1985 by
Book Club Associates
By arrangement with Thorsons Publishers Limited

Printed and bound in Great Britain

CONTENTS

Photography/Styling by Sue Atkinson, Mike Roles Studios
Home Economist — Pamela Swyther
Tableware was kindly loaned by Peter Knight of
Beaconsfield and The Token House, Windsor.
Oriental screen kindly loaned
by O'Connor Brothers, Windsor.

INTRODUCTION

It has been a huge pleasure to write this book; hardly anyone has the opportunity to create 52 of the most delicious dinner menus you could possibly dream up and it has been fun. However, I did set myself some limits. I did not want to use ingredients which were difficult to purchase; I wanted to make gourmet set meals out of ingredients that were readily available. For example, I have not used sorrel, though sorrel soup is a French classic and I grow it in my own garden and use it in various dishes. To include it seemed unfair (although I did have a lapse in one recipe and offered spinach as an alternative). I have also not included the salad vegetable, rocket, though I am very addicted to it and use it all the time in the summer and autumn as part of a mixed green salad. I do strongly suggest, if you have a garden, you consider growing these two green vegetables, for they increase the range of dishes and flavours one can concoct in the kitchen.

There is another main area which I more or less totally ignored, I did not set out to omit saturated fats, sugar or salt. There are enough health food books around (in fact, I have written one), and people can worry too much about these issues. Most of us now cut down on fats, sugars and salt, and eat more dietary fibre. The trend is towards health for those who care about food. Vegetarians have a much healthier diet than meat eaters anyway and this is a vegetarian gourmet book.

No one is going to eat meals like this every day of his life. No one would want to, for a start, and certainly you would have a surfeit of good food if you ate even two of these meals in a week! Once a week is probably enough, therefore, on that one occasion it will not do anyone any harm to include a spoonful of caster sugar or whipped cream in the pud. The other point I must make is that it is impossible to make a good roux (the basis of sauces and much else) with wholemeal flour. You have to use plain flour and again, a few spoonsful are not going to hurt you. There is another excellent flour which can sometimes be used — besan or gram flour, made from chickpeas, which can be bought at all Indian shops and some wholefood shops.

While I have not been earnest in my pursuit of wholefoods throughout this book, I have tried to keep a balance in the meals between raw and cooked, rich and spartan, carbohydrate and protein and have attempted not to over-use eggs, cream and cheese.

This is, of course, a highly personal choice. This is my kind of food. Any restaurant serving dishes similar to these would become my favourite haunt if I could afford it. Nor have I allowed cost to deter me in my choices, although once you eliminate meat, poultry and fish you have erased the most expensive items. Spend the money you have saved on good cheese and excellent wine. Life is for living and food is one of the most sensual experiences of all.

You will notice I have followed the French custom of serving the cheese after the main course. This is because I enjoy eating cheese with salad. When you have as good a meal as this, you would not want to continue to dally at the end with more bits of cheese and thus end up overeating, which is what often happens. But by all means change the order if you prefer. You are the one who is going to enjoy these meals, so please understand that these are only suggestions. The cheese and wines chosen are those I feel would go well with the food, just as the menus include courses I feel will complement each other. But if you feel differently, there is no reason why you should not create your own menus from my seasonal choices.

Freshness and Quality

You cannot make a good meal out of inferior ingredients. Vegetables must be as fresh as possible and of the highest quality. If you are fortunate enough to be able to cook with vegetables just plucked from the garden, it is paradise. The fresher a vegetable, the more flavour and the higher its mineral and vitamin content. Therefore, plan your menus around food which is in season.

On the whole, avoid all tinned food. There are a few exceptions in this book. Tinned artichoke hearts and bottoms are useful to have, as is tinned salsify and it always seems to me that frozen broad beans are consistently good. But unlike most cooks, I prefer the flavour of tomato sauce made from fresh tomatoes (at any time of the year) rather than tinned Italian plum tomatoes. However, these tins are marvellously useful when the larder is empty of fresh vegetables.

Presentation

What a meal looks like is of great importance. If it is visually enticing, the palate becomes seduced even before the first mouthful.

It is not a bad idea to start collecting pieces of Victorian china, which can often be picked up cheaply at auctions, especially the odd pieces. Large platters are essential. Moulds and timbales can be turned out on them with the sauce poured around the base. Platters can also be used for some salads, where the design is as important as the flavours (eg, the Watercress and Orange Salad on page 67).

A change in food presentation was introduced with nouvelle cuisine. Instead of serving food from large dishes, each course was arranged into a design on individual plates, rather like an abstract painting. Quite often the visual picture is of stunning beauty. I have often done this with the first course, choosing ingredients of contrasting colour and shape (julienne strips of carrot with watercress). It is here that your imagination and ingenuity will come into play, as you add a tiny sprig of garnish that is not referred to in the recipe. However, do not overload the plate. Nouvelle cuisine is very austere; a small portion of food, a little sauce, a sprig of garnish and the picture is complete. Puddings and desserts can also often be prepared in individual glasses or ramekins.

In the dining room, I like soft light, even candlelight, but not so dim that I cannot see the food or my guests' facial expressions. Conversation, after all, is the end result of dinner parties, and in a sense, the main enjoyment. Good food and wine both relaxes the company and stimulates it.

The amounts given are for dinner parties of 6 or 8. In some recipes, you might consider the portions modest, but this is because I have thought of the meal as a whole and there is nothing more off-putting to the palate than huge mounds of food. My view is that a small quantity of very good food is far more satisfying than a large amount of mediocre food.

The ideas for the meals and many of the dishes are derived from the great classic cooks of the past: Hannah Glasse, Eliza Acton, Indian and Chinese traditions, the Mediterranean and France. No present-day cook can ignore the huge debt of gratitude owed to the life work of Elizabeth David or to her scholarly successor, Jane Grigson. I have also borrowed from restaurants where I have eaten well and adapted recipes for vegetarian enjoyment. There is no doubt in my mind that we can eat far better than the meat eaters and I think the following pages will prove it. Bon appetit!

COLIN SPENCER

WINTER MENUS

WINTER MENU 1

Artichoke Pâté	Ombretta Bianco (Veronese table wine)
Macaroni with Eggs and Herbs	Bardolino
Red Cabbage with Sweet and Sour Sauce	or a
Raw Spinach and Avocado Salad	Cabernet
Gorgonzola	
Mascarpone	
Fresh Pineapple in its Shell	

ARTICHOKE PÂTÉ

Preparation time: 15 minutes
Cooking time: 45 minutes
Chilling time: 12 hours

IMPERIAL (METRIC)	AMERICAN
6-8 large artichokes	*6-8 large artichokes*
2 tablespoonsful olive oil	*2 tablespoonsful olive oil*
1 tablespoonful wine vinegar	*1 tablespoonful wine vinegar*
Sea salt and freshly ground black pepper	*Sea salt and freshly ground black pepper*
Hot wholemeal toast to serve	*Hot wholewheat toast to serve*

1. Cut stalks off artichokes. Place in a large pan and cover with water. Boil for 45 minutes and leave to cool.
2. Remove the leaves from the artichokes and scrape the edible flesh at the bottom of each leaf into a bowl. Discard the choke. Cut out the artichoke bottom and add it to the flesh in the bowl.
3. Blend the artichoke flesh into the oil and vinegar and season to taste.
4. Place the artichoke mixture into a suitable mould and refrigerate for 12 hours.
5. Turn out onto a serving dish and accompany with hot wholemeal toast.

MACARONI WITH EGGS AND HERBS

Preparation time: 5 minutes
Cooking time: 15 minutes

IMPERIAL (METRIC)	AMERICAN
1 lb (450g) macaroni	*1 lb macaroni*
5 eggs	*5 eggs*
1 tablespoonful water	*1 tablespoonful water*
1 tablespoonful olive oil	*1 tablespoonful olive oil*
Handful of finely chopped fresh parsley, mint and basil	*Handful of finely chopped fresh parsley, mint and basil*
2 oz (55g) freshly grated parmesan cheese	*½ cupful freshly grated parmesan cheese*
Sea salt and freshly ground black pepper	*Sea salt and freshly ground black pepper*

1. Cook the macaroni in plenty of salted, boiling water until *al dente* — about 8 minutes. Drain, pour into an earthenware dish and keep warm in a cool oven (250°F/130°C/Gas Mark ½).
2. Beat the eggs with the tablespoonful of water.
3. Heat the oil in a large frying pan. Pour in the eggs, then the herbs. Beat with a fork as if making scrambled eggs. When the eggs are almost done, remove from the heat.
4. Pour the eggs over the macaroni. Mix well to incorporate into the pasta.
5. Add the parmesan cheese and seasoning to taste and serve hot.

RED CABBAGE WITH SWEET AND SOUR SAUCE

Preparation time: 15 minutes
Cooking time: 15 minutes
Baking time: 3 hours

IMPERIAL (METRIC)	AMERICAN
1 medium-sized red cabbage	*1 medium-sized red cabbage*

Sauce:

IMPERIAL (METRIC)	AMERICAN
1 large onion, sliced	*1 large onion, sliced*
1 carrot, grated	*1 carrot, grated*
1 tablespoonful olive oil	*1 tablespoonful olive oil*
3 tablespoonsful cider vinegar	*3 tablespoonsful cider vinegar*
3 tablespoonsful soy sauce	*3 tablespoonsful soy sauce*
3 tablespoonsful water	*3 tablespoonsful water*
1 tablespoonful sultanas	*1 tablespoonful golden seedless raisins*
1 tablespoonful broken almonds	*1 tablespoonful broken almonds*
1 teaspoonful crushed cloves	*1 teaspoonful crushed cloves*
2 tablespoonsful honey	*2 tablespoonsful honey*
3 tablespoonsful grated bitter chocolate	*3 tablespoonsful grated bitter chocolate*

1. Slice the cabbage thinly. Place in a large ovenproof casserole. Preheat the oven to 350°F/180°C (Gas Mark 4).
2. Prepare the sauce. Gently cook the onion and carrot in the oil until soft, 3-5 minutes.
3. Add the vinegar, soy sauce, water, sultanas (golden seedless raisins), almonds, cloves and honey.
4. Stir well and simmer the sauce for 5 minutes.
5. Add the chocolate. Stir and let the sauce thicken a little.
6. Taste to check flavour. (The sauce may need more honey or vinegar or a little of both.)
7. Pour the sauce over the cabbage in the casserole and bake for 3 hours.
8. Remove the casserole from the oven. Stir well before serving.

RAW SPINACH AND AVOCADO SALAD
Preparation time: 10 minutes

IMPERIAL (METRIC)	AMERICAN
1 lb (450g) young spinach leaves	*1 lb young spinach leaves*
4 tablespoonsful olive oil	*4 tablespoonsful olive oil*
1 clove garlic, crushed	*1 clove garlic, crushed*
1 tablespoonful lemon juice	*1 tablespoonful lemon juice*
3 ripe avocados	*3 ripe avocados*
4 oz (115g) black olives	*1 cupful black olives*

1. Tear the spinach leaves from the stalks and discard the stalks. Cut the leaves into small strips.
2. Place the spinach in a large bowl. Mix the olive oil, garlic and lemon juice together and pour over the spinach. Mix well.
3. Peel and stone the avocados. Slice the flesh and add to the spinach. Mix thoroughly, but carefully to avoid breaking up the avocado flesh.
4. Add the olives and serve.

FRESH PINEAPPLE IN ITS SHELL
Preparation time: 15 minutes

IMPERIAL (METRIC)	AMERICAN
2 large, ripe pineapples	*2 large, ripe pineapples*
¼ pint (150ml) white rum	*⅔ cupful white rum*

1. Keeping the leaves of the pineapple intact, slice it in half vertically, then in half again.
2. Remove the hard central core from each quarter and discard it.
3. Cut the pineapple flesh vertically with a knife at regular intervals, almost down to the skin.
4. Place on individual plates or in 1 large bowl and sprinkle the rum evenly over each section.

WINTER MENU 2

Poached Eggs on Potato Purée	Sauvignon
Spiced Vegetable Risotto	Beaujolais or
Carrot Salad with Oranges	a young red
Bleu de Bresse	
Caerphilly	
Cinnamon Apples	Brandy

POACHED EGGS ON POTATO PURÉE

Preparation time: 15 minutes
Cooking time: 30 minutes

IMPERIAL (METRIC)	AMERICAN
2 lb (900g) potatoes	*2 lb potatoes*
2 oz (55g) butter or margarine	*4 tablespoonsful butter or margarine*
2 cloves garlic, crushed	*2 cloves garlic, crushed*
Pinch of nutmeg	*Pinch of nutmeg*
Sea salt and freshly ground black pepper	*Sea salt and freshly ground black pepper*
10 oz (285g) grated gruyère cheese	*2½ cupsful grated unprocessed gruyère cheese*
½ pint (300ml) single cream	*1¼ cupsful light cream*
4 oz (115g) finely chopped parsley	*2 cupsful finely chopped parsley*
6-8 eggs	*6-8 eggs*
4 oz (115g) freshly grated parmesan cheese	*1 cupful freshly grated parmesan cheese*

1. Peel the potatoes and boil in plenty of water. When cooked, drain well.
2. Mash the potatoes and place the pan back on the heat to remove any excess moisture, stirring well to avoid burning.
3. Add butter or margarine, garlic, nutmeg, salt, pepper, gruyère cheese and cream.
4. Continue to stir over the heat until the cheese has melted and the potato mixture begins to thicken. Remove from the heat and stir in the parsley.
5. Butter 6-8 individual ramekin dishes or one large flat oval dish. Place a portion of the potato purée in the bottom of each dish (or smooth it over the base of the large dish). Keep warm in a cool oven (250°F/130°C/Gas Mark ½).
6. Poach the eggs so that the whites are just set, but the yolks are still runny.
7. Slide one poached egg into each ramekin. Sprinkle a little grated parmesan cheese over the top and put it back into the oven to melt. Serve immediately.

SPICED VEGETABLE RISOTTO

Preparation time: 15 minutes
Cooking time: 10 minutes
Baking time: 45 minutes

IMPERIAL (METRIC)	AMERICAN
1 large aubergine	*1 large eggplant*
2 courgettes	*2 zucchini*
4 tablespoonsful olive oil	*4 tablespoonsful olive oil*
1 teaspoonful each: crushed cumin and coriander seeds, paprika and garam masala	*1 teaspoonful each: crushed cumin and coriander seeds, paprika and garam masala*
2 large onions, sliced	*2 large onions, sliced*
5 large cloves garlic, crushed	*5 large cloves garlic, crushed*
Sea salt and freshly ground black pepper	*Sea salt and freshly ground black pepper*
¾ lb (340g) rice	*1½ cupsful rice*
¼ pint (150ml) white wine or vermouth	*⅔ cupful white wine or vermouth*
1½ pints (900ml) boiling water	*4 cupsful boiling water*
2 tablespoonsful green peppercorns	*2 tablespoonsful green peppercorns*
1 oz (30g) butter	*2 tablespoonsful butter*
4 oz (115g) freshly grated parmesan cheese	*1 cupful freshly grated parmesan cheese*

1. Cut the aubergines (eggplants) and courgettes (zucchini) into small cubes.
2. Heat the oil in a heavy ovenproof pan and sauté all the spices. Add the aubergine, courgette, onion and garlic and cook gently for about 4 minutes, or until soft.
3. Add the salt, pepper and rice. Stir until the rice has soaked up all the oil and juices.
4. Remove the pan from the heat. Add the wine or vermouth, boiling water and green peppercorns.
5. Preheat the oven to 375°F/190°C (Gas Mark 5). Place the rice mixture in the oven and bake until the rice is cooked through, about 45 minutes.
6. Before serving, stir in the butter and parmesan cheese.

CARROT SALAD WITH ORANGES

Preparation time: 15 minutes
Standing time: 1 hour

IMPERIAL (METRIC)	AMERICAN
2 tablespoonsful olive oil	*2 tablespoonsful olive oil*
1 clove garlic, crushed	*1 clove garlic, crushed*
Juice of 1 lemon	*Juice of 1 lemon*
½ teaspoonful orange essence	*½ teaspoonful orange extract*
1 teaspoonful sea salt	*1 teaspoonful sea salt*
½ teaspoonful white pepper	*½ teaspoonful white pepper*
1¾ lb (790g) carrots	*1¾ lb carrots*
4 large oranges	*4 large oranges*

1. Mix oil, garlic, lemon juice, orange essence, salt and pepper together in a bowl.
2. Peel the carrots and grate into the bowl containing the dressing.
3. Using a small grater or a zest knife, take the zest from 2 of the oranges and add to the carrots.
4. Peel all the oranges and carefully remove all the white pith. Slice the oranges and add to the carrots.
5. Mix well and leave for an hour to absorb flavours.

CINNAMON APPLES

Preparation time: 10 minutes
Cooking time: 7 minutes

IMPERIAL (METRIC)	AMERICAN
2 lb (900g) cooking apples	*2 lb cooking apples*
2 oz (55g) butter or margarine	*4 tablespoonsful butter or margarine*
2 oz (55g) muscovado sugar	*⅓ cupful dark brown sugar*
1 tablespoonful ground cinnamon	*1 tablespoonful ground cinnamon*
¼ pint (150ml) double cream, whipped	*⅔ cupful heavy cream, whipped*

1. Core the apples, but do not pare them. Chop coarsely.
2. Melt the butter in a frying pan and add the apples. Sauté for 3-5 minutes, until they begin to soften.
3. Mix the sugar with the cinnamon and sprinkle over the apples. Cook, stirring well, for another 2 minutes.
4. Turn the apples into a bowl to cool slightly.
5. Pile the whipped cream on top of the warm apples and serve.

```
┌─────────────────────────────────────────────────────────┐
```

WINTER MENU 3

Endive, Orange and   Verdicchio dei
Pistachio Salad   Castelli ji Jesi

Courgettes Stuffed with Smoked Aubergine   Valpolicella
Haricots Blanc with Shallot

Emmental
Chèvre

Purée de Marrons   Marc

```
└─────────────────────────────────────────────────────────┘
```

ENDIVE, ORANGE AND PISTACHIO SALAD

Preparation time: 20 minutes

IMPERIAL (METRIC)	AMERICAN
1 endive	*1 head chicory*
4 oranges	*4 oranges*
½ lb (225g) pistachio nuts	*2 cupsful pistachio nuts*

Mayonnaise:	
2 egg yolks at room temperature	*2 egg yolks at room temperature*
1 teaspoonful mustard powder	*1 teaspoonful powdered mustard*
½ pint (300ml) olive oil	*1¼ cupsful olive oil*
Sea salt and freshly ground black	*Sea salt and freshly ground black*
pepper	*pepper*

1. Wash the endive (chicory) and cut the fronds from the central stalk. Peel the oranges, making sure to remove all the white pith. Slice the oranges into semicircles, reserving the juice. Shell the pistachio nuts.
2. Arrange the endive (chicory) on individual salad plates, with the white stalks in the centre of the plate and the feathery green edges on the outside edge of the plate. Place the orange slices over the endive (chicory), around the outside edge of the plate, leaving the centre free. Pile the pistachio nuts in the centre.
3. To make the mayonnaise, place the egg yolks in a bowl with the mustard and mix well. Add the olive oil slowly, drop by drop, stirring with a wire whisk or wooden spoon. Continue stirring and amalgamating the oil and egg, until all the oil is used up (it should be a thick paste). Thin it with about 2 tablespoonful of the reserved orange juice and season with salt and pepper.
4. Place a generous spoonful of mayonnaise over the nuts in the centre of the salad.

Note: This salad can be prepared an hour in advance. The mayonnaise will keep perfectly well if it is put into a bowl and covered, but do not refrigerate. Spoon the mayonnaise onto the salad just before serving.

COURGETTES STUFFED WITH SMOKED AUBERGINE

Preparation time: 20 minutes
Cooking time: 20 minutes

IMPERIAL (METRIC)	AMERICAN
1 large aubergine	*1 large eggplant*
6-8 medium-sized courgettes	*6-8 medium-sized zucchini*
10 cloves garlic	*10 cloves garlic*
8 tablespoonsful corn oil	*½ cupful corn oil*
¾ lb (340g) diced onion	*2 cupsful diced onion*
1 green chilli, deseeded and chopped	*1 green chili pepper, seeded and chopped*
2 tablespoonsful peeled, grated root ginger	*2 tablespoonsful peeled, grated ginger root*
1 1-lb (450g) tin tomatoes	*1 16-oz can tomatoes*
Juice of 1 lemon	*Juice of 1 lemon*
Sea salt and freshly ground black pepper	*Sea salt and freshly ground black pepper*
2 oz (55g) freshly grated parmesan cheese	*½ cupful freshly grated parmesan cheese*

1. Pierce the aubergine (eggplant) with two forks and hold it over a flame. (A gas ring will do, or alternatively, an electric hob.) Let the skin burn and blacken and come loose from the flesh within. Rotate the aubergine until the skin is completely charred and you can peel it away. Cut the flesh into cubes.
2. Cut each courgette (zucchini) in half lengthways and scoop out the seeds, leaving a boatlike indentation with flesh around it.
3. Peel the garlic cloves, chop 6 of them finely and crush the rest. Heat 4 tablespoonsful oil in a frying pan, put in the garlic, onion, chilli and ginger and sauté for about 3 minutes. Add the aubergine (eggplant) and continue to cook for another 2 minutes, then add the drained tomatoes (but save the juice from the tin), lemon juice, salt and pepper. Stir well, cover the pan, reduce the heat and simmer for up to 15 minutes. If the mixture sticks and gets too dry, add a little reserved tomato juice.
4. Heat the rest of the oil in another frying pan and sauté the courgettes, cut side down, until golden, then turn them over and sauté the other side. Do not allow them to get limp. They must still have a bite to them. Do them in batches and keep the already sautéed courgettes warm in a cool oven (250°F/130°C/Gas Mark ½).
5. Fill each courgette boat with some of the aubergine mixture and sprinkle the tops with the parmesan cheese. Place under a hot grill to brown.

Note: This recipe can be prepared in advance and placed under the grill at the last moment.

HARICOTS BLANC WITH SHALLOTS

Soaking time: overnight or 1 hour
Cooking time: 1 hour, plus reheating time
Standing time: 1 hour

IMPERIAL (METRIC)	AMERICAN
13 oz (370g) dried haricot beans	*2 cupsful dried navy beans*
2 tablespoonsful olive oil	*2 tablespoonsful olive oil*
1 teaspoonful ground cumin	*1 teaspoonful ground cumin*
1 teaspoonful ground fennel	*1 teaspoonful ground fennel*
6 oz (170g) diced shallots	*1 cupful diced shallots*
Sea salt and freshly ground black pepper	*Sea salt and freshly ground black pepper*

1. Soak the beans overnight in plenty of water, or pour boiling water over them to cover and leave for 1 hour.
2. Heat the oil in a saucepan, add the cumin, fennel and shallots. Sauté for a minute or two, then add the well-drained beans. Stir well and continue to sauté for another minute or two, then add enough water to cover the beans by 2 inches (5cm). Bring to the boil and simmer for 1 hour. Watch carefully and add more liquid if necessary.
3. If the beans are done and all the liquid is absorbed, turn off the heat. (It is impossible to give exact cooking times for dried vegetables, for some may soak up more water than others.) Add salt and pepper to taste and let the beans rest for 1 hour to soak up the flavours.
4. Reheat the beans before serving.

PURÉE DE MARRONS

Preparation time: 20 minutes
Chilling time: 1 hour

IMPERIAL (METRIC)	AMERICAN
1 31-oz (870g) tin unsweetened chestnut purée	*1 31-oz can unsweetened chestnut purée*
2½ fl oz (75ml) dry sherry	*⅓ cupful dry sherry*
1 tablespoonful muscovado sugar	*1 tablespoonful dark brown sugar*
5 eggs, separated	*5 eggs, separated*
1 pint (600ml) double cream	*2½ cupsful heavy cream*
½ lb (225g) marrons glacé, finely sliced	*1 cupful marrons glacé, finely sliced*

1. Pour the chestnut purée into a large mixing bowl. Add the sherry and sugar. Mix well. Add the egg yolks.
2. Place the egg whites in a bowl and whisk until stiff. Stir the egg whites gently into the chestnut mixture until they are all absorbed.
3. Whip the cream until thick. Add to the chestnuts, reserving a small amount to use for decorating.
4. Pile the mixture into a serving bowl or into individual glasses. Chill for 1 hour.
5. Just before serving, decorate the purée with the sliced marrons glacé, then top with whipped cream.

WINTER MENU 4

Celeriac Remoulade in Pastry Case	Orvieto
Walnut Risotto **Cauliflower with Broad Beans**	Rioja
Blue Wensleydale **Bel Paese**	
Petits Pots au Chocolat	Brandy

CELERIAC REMOULADE IN PASTRY CASE

Preparation time: 30 minutes
Chilling time: 1-24 hours
Baking time: 20 minutes

IMPERIAL (METRIC)	AMERICAN
Pastry:	
¾ lb (340g) plain flour	*3 cupsful all-purpose flour*
½ teaspoonful salt	*½ teaspoonful salt*
6 oz (170g) butter or margarine	*¾ cupful butter or margarine*
2-4 tablespoonsful iced water	*2-4 tablespoonsful ice water*
Mayonnaise:	
2 egg yolks at room temperature	*2 egg yolks at room temperature*
½ teaspoonful wine vinegar	*½ teaspoonful wine vinegar*
½ pint (300ml) olive oil	*1½ cupsful olive oil*
Sea salt and freshly ground black pepper	*Sea salt and freshly ground black pepper*
1 large celeriac	*1 large celeriac*
6-8 stoned black olives	*6-8 pitted black olives*

1. Sift the flour with the salt and crumble the butter or margarine into it. Add the iced water and mould pastry into two balls. Cover with cling film and refrigerate for a day, or even just an hour.
2. Make the mayonnaise. Using the ingredients listed here, prepare as in mayonnaise recipe on page 19.
3. Roll out the pastry for 6-8 individual tartlet cases or 2 large (8-inch/20cm) tart cases. Bake blind in a preheated oven at 400°F/200°C (Gas Mark 6) for 15-20 minutes. Remove tart cases from the oven and allow to cool.

22

4. Pare the celeriac root and grate the flesh into a bowl. Cover with boiling water and drain well after 1 minute. Let the celeriac cool, then drain again. Pat dry with a clean cloth and mix with the mayonnaise.

5. Fill each pastry case with some of the celeriac mixture. Decorate each tart with a black olive.

WALNUT RISOTTO

Cooking time: 10 minutes
Baking time: 40 minutes

IMPERIAL (METRIC)	AMERICAN
3 tablespoonsful olive oil	*3 tablespoonsful olive oil*
1 small savoy cabbage, sliced	*1 small savoy cabbage, sliced*
6 cloves garlic, crushed	*6 cloves garlic, crushed*
1 lb (450g) rice	*2 cupsful rice*
½ lb (225g) chopped walnuts	*2 cupsful chopped walnuts*
Sea salt and freshly ground black pepper	*Sea salt and freshly ground black pepper*
2 oz (55g) butter	*4 tablespoonsful butter*
4 oz (115g) freshly grated parmesan cheese	*1 cupful freshly grated parmesan cheese*

1. Heat the oil in an ovenproof pan with a tightly fitting lid and sauté the cabbage and garlic together for a few minutes.

2. Add the rice, stirring it so that it soaks up the oil and juices. Add the chopped walnuts and enough water to cover the ingredients in the pan plus 1 inch (2.5cm). Season with salt and pepper.

3. Preheat the oven to 350°F/180°C (Gas Mark 4). Cover the pan and place in the oven for 40 minutes.

4. Stir in the butter and parmesan cheese just before serving.

CAULIFLOWER WITH BROAD BEANS

Preparation time: 10 minutes
Cooking time: 20 minutes

IMPERIAL (METRIC)	AMERICAN
1 large or 2 small cauliflowers	*1 large or 2 small cauliflowers*
1 lb (450g) frozen broad beans	*1 lb frozen fava beans*
2 tablespoonsful olive oil	*2 tablespoonsful olive oil*
1 teaspoonful crushed coriander seeds	*1 teaspoonful crushed coriander seeds*
Juice of 1 lemon	*Juice of 1 lemon*
2 tablespoonsful water	*2 tablespoonsful water*
¼ pint (150ml) natural yogurt	*⅔ cupful plain yogurt*
Sea salt and freshly ground black pepper	*Sea salt and freshly ground black pepper*

1. Separate the cauliflower into florets and dice the central core into bite-sized pieces.
2. Cook the beans in boiling water until they are just tender. Drain and reserve.
3. Heat the olive oil in a saucepan and add the coriander and cauliflower. Turn the cauliflower in the oil and spice for a moment, then add the lemon juice and water. Cover the saucepan, reduce the heat and simmer for 5 minutes.
4. Increase the heat a little and add the broad beans. Stir well, then add the yogurt, salt and pepper, stirring well. Cover the pan and gently reheat for about 2 minutes. Serve immediately.

Note: This dish can be made in advance and reheated just before serving.

PETITS POTS AU CHOCOLAT

Preparation time: 10 minutes
Chilling time: 4 hours

IMPERIAL (METRIC)	AMERICAN
1 lb (450g) plain or bitter chocolate	*1 lb semisweet or bitter chocolate*
1 pint (600ml) single cream	*2½ cupsful light cream*
1 teaspoonful salt	*1 teaspoonful salt*
¾ teaspoonful vanilla essence	*¾ teaspoonful vanilla extract*
2 eggs	*2 eggs*

1. Break the chocolate into a blender container.
2. Scald the cream and just before it boils, pour it onto the chocolate and turn the blender on. Add the salt, vanilla essence and eggs. Continue to blend until smooth.
3. Pour into 6-8 small ramekins and chill for 4 hours before serving.

Opposite: Okra Stew (page 40).
Overleaf: Winter Menu 7 (pages 32 to 34).

WINTER MENU 5

Brussels Sprouts and Chestnut Soup	Fendant du Valais
Stuffed Peppers **Gratin Dauphinoise** **Turnip and Fennel Salad**	Côtes-du-Rhône Villages
Gaperon **Cheddar**	
Platter of Tropical Fruits	Eau de Vie

BRUSSELS SPROUTS AND CHESTNUT SOUP

Soaking time: overnight
Preparation time: 15 minutes
Cooking time: 1 hour, plus reheating time

IMPERIAL (METRIC)	AMERICAN
4 oz (115g) dried chestnuts	*⅔ cupful dried chestnuts*
2½ pints (1.5 litres) water	*6 cupsful water*
1 lb (450g) Brussels sprouts	*1 lb Brussels sprouts*
¼ pint (150ml) soured cream	*⅔ cupful sour cream*
Sea salt and freshly ground black *pepper*	*Sea salt and freshly ground black* *pepper*

1. Soak chestnuts overnight in the water.
2. Drain the soaking water into a saucepan. Pick over the chestnuts and remove any skin that adheres to them. Drop the chestnuts into the saucepan and bring to the boil. Simmer for 1 hour.
3. Remove the chestnuts from the pan with a slotted spoon and put into a blender. Make up the water again to 2½ pints/1.5 litres/6 cupsful.
4. Bring the water to the boil and cook the Brussels sprouts for 5 minutes. Remove from the heat and cool.
5. Add the Brussels sprouts and cooking liquor to the chestnuts in the blender. Add the sour cream and blend to a purée. Season with salt and pepper.
6. Reheat gently, but do not let the soup boil.

Opposite: Götterspiese (page 38).

STUFFED PEPPERS

Preparation time: 20 minutes
Cooking time: 50 minutes

IMPERIAL (METRIC)	AMERICAN
6-8 medium-sized green peppers	*6-8 medium-sized green peppers*
4 oz (115g) mushrooms	*¼ lb mushrooms*
¾ lb (340g) onions	*¾ lb onions*
3 cloves garlic, crushed	*3 cloves garlic, crushed*
2 large carrots	*2 large carrots*
Zest and juice of 1 lemon	*Zest and juice of 1 lemon*
2 oz (55g) chopped celery leaves	*1 cupful chopped celery leaves*
2 oz (55g) chopped parsley	*1 cupful chopped parsley*
1 teaspoonful chopped dillweed	*1 teaspoonful chopped dillweed*
4 oz (115g) grated parmesan cheese	*1 cupful grated parmesan cheese*
4 oz (115g) grated gruyère cheese	*1 cupful grated unprocessed gruyère cheese*
2 tablespoonsful olive oil	*2 tablespoonsful olive oil*
Sea salt and freshly ground black pepper	*Sea salt and freshly ground black pepper*

1. Prepare the vegetables. Cut the tops off the peppers, remove the seeds and pith and discard. Set aside the peppers and lids. Chop the mushrooms and onions and place in a bowl with the garlic. Grate the carrots and place in another bowl with the lemon zest, celery leaves, parsley, dillweed, parmesan and gruyère cheese.
2. Heat the oil in a frying pan and sauté the mushrooms, onions and garlic until the mushrooms are soft and have released some of their moisture. Remove from the heat and add to the carrot mixture. Mix well and season with salt and pepper.
3. Fill the reserved peppers with the stuffing and place them into a saucepan that will just hold them upright. Place the lids on the peppers and squeeze the lemon juice over. Pour enough water into the saucepan to come halfway up the sides of the peppers.
4. Simmer the peppers for about 45 minutes, remove from the pan with a slotted spoon and keep warm in the oven for a moment or two before serving.

Note: The liquid left in the pan makes a good stock for soups.

GRATIN DAUPHINOISE

Preparation time: 15 minutes
Soaking time: 30 minutes
Baking time: 2½ hours

IMPERIAL (METRIC)	AMERICAN
2 lb (900g) potatoes	*2 lb potatoes*
2 oz (55g) butter, softened	*4 tablespoonsful butter, softened*
1 teaspoonful grated nutmeg	*1 teaspoonful grated nutmeg*
Sea salt and freshly ground black pepper	*Sea salt and freshly ground black pepper*
2 pints (1.2 litres) single cream	*5 cupsful light cream*

1. Peel the potatoes and slice, either on a mandoline, or in a food processor.
2. Soak the potato slices in cold water for 30 minutes. Drain well, then pat dry.
3. Smear a shallow earthenware dish with the butter. Place a layer of sliced potatoes on the bottom and season with nutmeg, salt and pepper. Continue layering the potatoes and seasoning in the dish until half the ingredients have been used.
4. Pour over half the cream and wait for a moment or two until the cream runs down into the bottom of the dish, then add the remainder of the potatoes and seasoning. Pour in the rest of the cream.
5. Place the dish into a preheated oven 300°F/150°C (Gas Mark 2) and bake for about 2½ hours.

TURNIP AND FENNEL SALAD

Preparation time: 15 minutes
Cooking time: 4 minutes

IMPERIAL (METRIC)	AMERICAN
1 lb (450g) small turnips	*1 lb small turnips*
2 fennel bulbs	*2 fennel bulbs*
2 oz (55g) flaked almonds, toasted	*½ cupful slivered almonds, toasted*

Vinaigrette Dressing:

3 tablespoonsful olive oil	*3 tablespoonsful olive oil*
1 teaspoonful cider vinegar	*1 teaspoonful cider vinegar*
Sea salt and freshly ground black pepper	*Sea salt and freshly ground black pepper*
2 oz (55g) chopped parsley to garnish	*1 cupful chopped parsley to garnish*

1. Cut the turnips into quarters and boil them in a little salted water for about 4 minutes, or until just tender.
2. Slice the fennel thinly.
3. Mix the oil, vinegar and seasoning together.
4. Place the turnips, fennel and almonds in a salad bowl. Just before serving, toss with the vinaigrette and sprinkle the parsley on top.

PLATTER OF TROPICAL FRUITS

For a good variety, choose mangoes, guavas, passion fruit, papaya, lychees, pineapple, mandarins and clementines. Arrange attractively on a serving dish. Nothing looks more delicious or pleases guests so much. Let them help themselves.

WINTER MENU 6

Avocado with Spring Onions and Soured Cream   Graves

Fennel and Cauliflower Pie   Beaujolais
Caramelized Carrots
Green Salad

Chèvre
Cheddar

Orange and Cinnamon Cream   Calvados

AVOCADO WITH SPRING ONIONS AND SOURED CREAM
Preparation time: 15 minutes

IMPERIAL (METRIC)	AMERICAN
1 teaspoonful garam masala	*1 teaspoonful garam masala*
Sea salt and freshly ground black pepper	*Sea salt and freshly ground black pepper*
Juice of 1 lemon	*Juice of 1 lemon*
½ pint (300ml) soured cream	*1¼ cupsful sour cream*
2 bunches spring onions	*2 bunches scallions*
3-4 ripe avocados	*3-4 ripe avocados*
Green lettuce leaves to garnish	*Green lettuce leaves to garnish*

1. Mix the garam masala, salt, pepper and lemon juice together in a bowl. Add the soured cream and mix well.
2. Trim the spring onions and chop them finely, using all of the green part that is edible. Add to the soured cream mixture.
3. Cut the avocados in half and remove the stones. Pile the soured cream mixture into the cavities.
4. Serve on a bed of lettuce leaves.

FENNEL AND CAULIFLOWER PIE

Preparation time:	25 minutes
Chilling time:	30 minutes
Cooking time:	12 minutes
Baking time:	50 minutes

IMPERIAL (METRIC)
Pastry:
½ lb (225g) plain flour
½ lb (225g) wholemeal flour
1 teaspoonful salt
2 oz (55g) butter or margarine
2 oz (55g) solid vegetable fat
4-5 tablespoonsful water

Filling:
1 large cauliflower
2 fennel bulbs
*1 tablespoonful Meaux mustard (or
   other strong mustard)*
2 tablespoonsful soy sauce
¼ pint (150ml) water
2 teaspoonsful arrowroot
*Sea salt and freshly ground black
   pepper*
1 beaten egg to glaze pastry

AMERICAN

2 cupsful all-purpose flour
2 cupsful wholewheat flour
1 teaspoonful salt
4 tablespoonsful butter or margarine
*4 tablespoonsful vegetable
   shortening*
4-5 tablespoonsful water

1 large cauliflower
2 fennel bulbs
*1 tablespoonful Meaux mustard (or
   other strong mustard)*
2 tablespoonsful soy sauce
⅔ cupful water
2 teaspoonsful arrowroot
*Sea salt and freshly ground black
   pepper*
1 beaten egg to glaze pastry

1. Sift the flour and salt into a bowl. Cut the butter and fat into pieces and rub into the flour. (Or grate slightly frozen fat, then rub in) until the mixture resembles fine breadcrumbs. Add the water very gradually, stirring with a knife. When the dough holds together, form into two balls, cover with cling film and refrigerate for at least half an hour.

2. Separate the cauliflower into florets and cut the central core into julienne strips. Cut the fennel into quarters.

3. Place the cauliflower and fennel in a saucepan of boiling water and simmer for only 4-5 minutes. Both vegetables should have plenty of bite in them. Remove from the heat and drain well, reserving ¼ pint/150ml/⅔ cupful of the cooking liquor.

4. Grease a 12-inch (30cm) pie dish or two 8-inch (20cm) pie dishes. Take half the pastry dough out of the refrigerator and roll out. Fit it into the pie dish(es).

5. Preheat the oven to 400°F/200°C (Gas Mark 6) and bake the pastry blind for 10-15 minutes. Remove from the oven and allow to cool. Leave the oven on.

6. Mix the mustard, soy sauce and water together in a saucepan over a low heat, stir in the arrowroot and allow to thicken. Add the pepper and taste. The soy sauce should provide enough salt, but you may want to add just a bit more. You may also have to add more water, since the sauce should be no thicker than gravy.

7. Fit the cauliflower and fennel into the pie crust so that they are lying snugly together. Pour the sauce over, then roll out the remainder of the dough for the lid. Brush the top of the pastry with beaten egg.

8. Place the pie in the preheated oven and bake for 35-40 minutes.

CARAMELIZED CARROTS

Preparation time: 10 minutes
Cooking time: 25 minutes

IMPERIAL (METRIC)	AMERICAN
2 lb (900g) carrots	*2 lb carrots*
4 oz (115g) butter	*½ cupful (1 stick) butter*
2 oz (55g) raw cane sugar	*¼ cupful raw cane sugar*
Sea salt and freshly ground black	*Sea salt and freshly ground black*
pepper	*pepper*

1. Slice the carrots thinly on a mandoline or in a food processor.
2. Cook the carrots in slightly salted boiling water for 20 minutes, or until they are just done.
3. Drain the carrots well. Add the butter to the carrots in the saucepan, let it melt, then add the sugar. Over a low heat, turn the carrots over in the butter and sugar until the sugar has caramelized. (This will take about 3 minutes, depending on how hot the heat is.) Season to taste. The carrots may be kept warm in the oven for a while.

GREEN SALAD

A good green salad takes virtually no preparation time, but always choose a crisp lettuce. It is worse than useless to serve up those limp hothouse lettuces which are tasteless and indigestible. Use only the heart and discard all leaves that are damaged. Serve with the plainest vinaigrette. The purpose of the salad is to refresh the palate, not stimulate it any more. Keep the salad on the table while you are serving the cheese; many of us like to have the cheese with the salad and before the dessert.

ORANGE AND CINNAMON CREAM

Preparation time: 15 minutes
Chilling time: 30 minutes

IMPERIAL (METRIC)
4 large oranges
1 tablespoonful raw cane sugar
1 tablespoonful white rum, eau de
   vie or calvados

AMERICAN
4 large oranges
1 tablespoonful raw cane sugar
1 tablespoonful white rum, eau de
   vie or calvados

Cinnamon Cream:
1 pint (600ml) double cream
1 teaspoonful ground cinnamon
3 tablespoonsful raw cane sugar
4 egg whites

2½ cupsful heavy cream
1 teaspoonful ground cinnamon
3 tablespoonsful raw cane sugar
4 egg whites

1. Peel the oranges and remove all the pith and pips. Cut into slices and place in a serving bowl. Mix the sugar and spirits together and pour over the oranges.
2. Whip the cream until stiff, then fold in the cinnamon and sugar.
3. Whisk the egg whites until stiff. Fold into the cream mixture.
4. Pile the cinnamon cream on top of the oranges and refrigerate or keep cool for 30 minutes before serving.

WINTER MENU 7
(Illustrated between pages 24 and 25.)

Stuffed Lettuce Rolls with Beetroot Salad   Chardonnay

Mélange Bourguignonne   Saint-Emilion
Gratin Jurassien
Green Salad (See page 30)

Brie
Cheddar

Chocolate Yogurt Ambrosia   Marc or
Calvados

STUFFED LETTUCE ROLLS WITH BEETROOT SALAD

Preparation time: 25 minutes

IMPERIAL (METRIC)	AMERICAN
Beetroot salad:	
1 lb (450g) boiled beetroot	*1 lb boiled beets*
2 tablespoonsful olive oil	*2 tablespoonsful olive oil*
2 teaspoonsful raspberry vinegar	*2 teaspoonsful raspberry vinegar*
Sea salt and freshly ground black	*Sea salt and freshly ground black*
pepper	*pepper*
Lettuce rolls:	
1 tender round-heart lettuce	*1 Boston or butter lettuce*
8 oz (225g) curd cheese	*1 cupful cottage cheese*
2 tablespoonsful soured cream	*2 tablespoonsful sour cream*
1 bunch of spring onions, chopped	*1 bunch scallions, chopped*
Pinch of sea salt	*Pinch of sea salt*
Pinch of cayenne pepper	*Pinch of cayenne pepper*
Zest and juice of 1 lemon	*Zest and juice of 1 lemon*
1 clove garlic, crushed	*1 clove garlic, crushed*

1. Peel the beetroot, slice thinly and place in a serving bowl. Mix the oil, vinegar, salt and pepper together and pour over the beetroot.
2. Choose 6-8 good-sized lettuce leaves and blanch in boiling water for 1 minute. Drain well and pat dry.
3. Mix the cheese with the remainder of the ingredients. Spread a portion of the cheese mixture on each lettuce leaf and roll up into small parcels. (Roll the leaf over the filling once, then tuck in the end and continue to roll until it is neat.)
4. Place the bowl of beetroot salad on a serving platter and arrange the lettuce rolls around it.

MÉLANGE BOURGUIGNONNE

This recipe must be started 3 days in advance. It requires 2 separate overnight preparations, plus 2½ hours cooking time on the second day, then 2 hours standing time, plus approximately 1¾ hours cooking time on the third day.

IMPERIAL (METRIC)

Marinade:

¾ pint (450ml) red wine
4 tablespoonsful brandy
Sprig of fresh rosemary
12 whole peppercorns, crushed
12 juniper berries, crushed
1 teaspoonful sea salt
1 teaspoonful mustard powder

Mélange:

4 oz (115g) dried apricots
4 oz (115g) dried chickpeas
4 oz (115g) dried chestnuts
1 large aubergine
2 large onions
2 large carrots
10 cloves garlic
2 tablespoonsful olive oil
1 pint (600ml) vegetable stock
1 tablespoonful paprika
Zest and juice of 1 lemon
1 tablespoonful brown sugar
Sea salt and freshly ground black
  pepper

AMERICAN

2 cupsful red wine
4 tablespoonsful brandy
Sprig of fresh rosemary
12 whole peppercorns, crushed
12 juniper berries, crushed
1 teaspoonful sea salt
1 teaspoonful powdered mustard

¾ cupful dried apricots
½ cupful dried chick peas
  (garbanzo beans)
⅔ cupful dried chestnuts
1 large eggplant
2 large onions
2 large carrots
10 cloves garlic
2 tablespoonsful olive oil
2½ cupsful vegetable stock
1 tablespoonful paprika
Zest and juice of 1 lemon
1 tablespoonful brown sugar
Sea salt and freshly ground black
  pepper

1. Prepare the marinade and put the apricots in to soak.
2. Soak chickpeas (garbanzos) and chestnuts separately overnight.
3. Second day: Boil the chickpeas in plenty of water for 2 hours. Drain and add chickpeas to marinade.
4. Boil chestnuts for 30 minutes, pick over to remove remnants of skin and add the chestnuts to the marinade. Leave to marinate overnight.
5. Third day: Chop the aubergine into cubes, sprinkle with salt and leave for 2 hours. Rinse, drain and pat dry and add to marinade.
6. Slice the onions, carrots and garlic. Heat the oil in a thick-bottomed saucepan and cook the sliced vegetables for a moment or two, then add all the marinated ingredients, including the liquid and the vegetable stock, bring to the boil, then simmer for 1½ hours.
7. Remove from the heat and extract all the vegetables. Keep warm. Return the pan to the heat. Add the paprika, lemon zest and juice and sugar. Boil to reduce the stock to about ½ pint / 300ml / 1¼ cupsful. (It will thicken and become sticky.) Return the vegetables to the pan, mix into the sauce, season and serve.

GRATIN JURASSIEN

Preparation time: 15 minutes
Soaking time: 30 minutes
Baking time: 2 hours

IMPERIAL (METRIC)	AMERICAN
2 lb (900g) potatoes	*2 lb potatoes*
2 oz (55g) butter	*4 tablespoonsful butter*
Sea salt and freshly ground black pepper	*Sea salt and freshly ground black pepper*
½ lb (225g) grated gruyère cheese	*2 cupsful grated unprocessed gruyère cheese*
1 pint (600ml) single cream	*2½ cupsful light cream*

1. Peel the potatoes and slice, either on a mandoline, or in a food processor.
2. Soak the potato slices in cold water for 30 minutes, Drain well, then pat dry.
3. Grease a shallow ovenproof dish with a little of the butter. Place a layer of potatoes in the dish, dot with butter, season and sprinkle with some of the cheese. Continue to layer until the potatoes, butter and cheese are all used.
4. Pour the cream over the top and place the dish in an oven preheated to 300°F/150°C (Gas Mark 2). Bake for 2 hours.

CHOCOLATE YOGURT AMBROSIA

Preparation time: 10 minutes
Chilling time: overnight

IMPERIAL (METRIC)	AMERICAN
½ pint (300ml) natural yogurt	*1¼ cupsful plain yogurt*
½ pint (300ml) double cream	*1¼ cupsful heavy cream*
2 oz (55g) plain or bitter chocolate, grated	*½ cupful grated semisweet or bitter chocolate*
2 tablespoonsful soft brown sugar	*2 tablespoonsful soft brown sugar*

1. Whip the yogurt and cream together.
2. Fold the grated chocolate into the yogurt-cream mixture.
3. Pour into 6-8 ramekins or glasses and sprinkle the sugar on the top. Refrigerate overnight.

WINTER MENU 8

Malfati	Gewürtztraminer
Turnip Purée with Pine Nuts	Valpolicella
Artichoke Pie	
Watercress Salad with Endive and Cucumber	
Stilton	
Red Leicester	Cherry Brandy
	or Calvados
Götterspeise	

MALFATI (Parsley Gnocci)

Preparation time: overnight, plus 20 minutes
Cooking time: 15 minutes

IMPERIAL (METRIC)	AMERICAN
½ lb (225g) ricotta cheese	*½ lb ricotta cheese*
¾ lb (340g) finely chopped parsley	*¾ lb finely chopped parsley*
1 tablespoonful flour, sifted	*1 tablespoonful flour, sifted*
Sea salt and freshly ground black pepper	*Sea salt and freshly ground black pepper*
2 egg whites	*2 egg whites*
4 oz (115g) butter, melted	*½ cupful (1 stick) butter, melted*
3 oz (85g) freshly grated parmesan cheese	*¾ cupful freshly grated parmesan cheese*
3 oz (85g) freshly grated gruyère cheese	*¾ cupful freshly grated unprocessed gruyère cheese*

1. Make the gnocchi. Mash the ricotta cheese with the parsley, flour, salt and pepper and mix in the egg whites. Leave overnight.
2. Flour a pastry board and your hands. Shape the gnocchi mixture into small egg shapes and roll them in flour.
3. Pour the melted butter into an ovenproof dish, brushing the butter on the sides of the dish. Place in a cool oven 250°F/130°C (Gas Mark ½).
4. Fill a large saucepan with salted water and bring to the boil. Throw in a gnocchi one by one. When they rise to the surface, they are done. Remove with a slotted spoon and drain.
5. After each piece of gnocchi has been poached and drained, place it in the buttered dish and cover until all the gnocchi have been poached.
6. Increase the oven temperature to 300°F/150°C (Gas Mark 2). When the gnocchi are hot enough to serve, sprinkle with the parmesan and gruyère cheese, place back in the oven briefly, then serve immediately.

TURNIP PURÉE WITH PINE NUTS

Preparation time: 5 minutes
Cooking time: 10 minutes, plus reheating

IMPERIAL (METRIC)	AMERICAN
1 lb (450g) turnips	*1 lb turnips*
3 tablespoonsful pine nuts	*3 tablespoonsful pine nuts*
1 oz (30g) butter	*2 tablespoonsful butter*
1 tablespoonful double cream	*1 tablespoonful heavy cream*
Sea salt and white pepper	*Sea salt and white pepper*

1. Preheat the oven to 350°F/180°C (Gas Mark 4).
2. Quarter the turnips and cook them in a little boiling water until just soft, about 10 minutes.
3. In the meantime, spread the pine nuts on a baking tray, place in the oven and toast lightly, about 10 minutes. Remove from the oven and reduce the temperature slightly.
4. Remove the turnips from the heat. Drain well. Blend to a purée with the butter, cream, salt and pepper.
5. Place the purée in a shallow ovenproof dish, scatter the pine nuts on top and put the dish into the oven to reheat.
6. Serve with a little more butter melting on the top.

ARTICHOKE PIE

Defrosting time: 1 hour at room temperature or overnight in refrigerator
Preparation time: 15 minutes
Cooking time: 5 minutes
Baking time: 30 minutes, plus reheating

IMPERIAL (METRIC)	AMERICAN
¾ lb (340g) frozen puff pastry	*12 oz frozen puff pastry*
Filling:	
1 14-oz (395g) tin artichoke bottoms	*1 14-oz can artichoke bottoms*
½ lb (225g) mushrooms, thinly sliced	*½ lb mushrooms, thinly sliced*
4 hard-boiled egg yolks, chopped	*4 hard-boiled egg yolks, chopped*
Sauce:	
2 egg yolks, beaten	*2 egg yolks, beaten*
2 oz (55g) butter	*4 tablespoonsful butter*
2 tablespoonsful lemon juice	*2 tablespoonsful lemon juice*
4 tablespoonsful dry white wine	*4 tablespoonsful dry white wine*
Sea salt and freshly ground black pepper	*Sea salt and freshly ground black pepper*

1. Defrost the pastry, either by leaving it at room temperature for 1 hour, or placing it in the refrigerator overnight.

2. Roll out half the pastry and use it to line the bottom and sides of a 10-inch (25cm) pie dish.

3. Drain the artichoke bottoms well. Place a layer of artichokes into the pie shell, then a layer of mushrooms and finally, the egg yolks.

4. Roll out the remainder of the pastry for a lid, place on top of the filling, press down to seal and glaze the top of the pie with a little of the beaten egg to be used in the sauce.

5. Preheat the oven to 425°F/220°C (Gas Mark 7). Bake the pie for about 30 minutes or until the pastry is well-risen and golden.

6. Remove the pie from the oven and allow to cool a little. Reduce the oven temperature to 300°F/150°C (Gas Mark 2).

7. Make the sauce. Heat the butter in a small saucepan. Mix the egg yolks with the lemon juice in a small bowl or cup. Add the wine to the pan and let it heat up, then add the egg yolks and lemon juice, stirring continously.

8. Cut a large circle from the pastry lid and pour in the sauce. Replace the lid and reheat pie briefly in the oven before serving.

WATERCRESS SALAD WITH ENDIVE AND CUCUMBER

Preparation time: 15 minutes
Standing time: 1 hour

IMPERIAL (METRIC)	AMERICAN
1 cucumber	*1 cucumber*
2 bunches watercress	*2 bunches watercress*
2-3 endives	*2-3 heads chicory*

Vinaigrette dressing:

1 teaspoonful Meaux or Dijon	*1 teaspoonful Meaux or Dijon*
mustard	*mustard*
1 tablespoonful lemon juice	*1 tablespoonful lemon juice*
Sea salt and freshly ground black	*Sea salt and freshly ground black*
pepper	*pepper*
4 tablespoonsful olive oil	*4 tablespoonsful olive oil*
2 tablespoonsful chopped fresh	*2 tablespoonsful chopped fresh*
fennel (feathery tops) or parsley	*fennel (feathery tops) or parsley*

1. Slice cucumber very thinly on a mandoline and place into a bowl of salted water. Leave for an hour.

2. Chop the stalks off the watercress and discard. Wash the leaves well. Separate the fronds of endive and discard the central core.

3. Make the vinaigrette. Mix the mustard and lemon juice together, add the salt, pepper and olive oil.

4. Drain all the salad vegetables and pat dry.

5. Arrange the endive (chicory) on the outside edges of a large platter, like the spokes of a wheel, pile the watercress in the centre and arrange the cucumber slices between the watercress and endive. Scatter the fennel or parsley over the endive and cucumber.

6. Just before serving, pour a little of the dressing on the salad. Bring the remainder of the dressing to the table for guests to help themselves.

GÖTTERSPEISE (Food of the Gods)

(Illustrated opposite page 25.)

Preparation time: 10 minutes
Cooking time: 10 minutes

IMPERIAL (METRIC)
½ lb (225g) cranberries
2 tablespoonsful water
3 oz (85g) raw cane sugar
6 oz (170g) pumpernickel bread,
   cubed
½ pint (300ml) whipping cream
1 tablespoonful caster or icing sugar
3 oz (85g) plain or bitter chocolate,
   grated

AMERICAN
½ lb cranberries
2 tablespoonsful water
½ cupful raw cane sugar
6 slices pumpernickel bread, cubed
1¼ cupsful whipping cream
1 tablespoonful superfine or
   confectioner's sugar
¾ cupful semisweet or bitter
   chocolate, grated

1. Cook the cranberries with the water and sugar until just soft. Leave to cool.
2. Put the bread into an electric blender and reduce to crumbs.
3. Pour the breadcrumbs into the bottom of a glass serving dish. Spoon the cranberries on top of the crumbs.
4. Whip the cream and sugar together and spread over the cranberries.
5. Sprinkle the grated chocolate over the cream.

WINTER MENU 9

Middle Eastern Egg and Vegetable Salad	Demestica White
Moroccan Potato Casserole Okra Stew Courgette Rissoles Green Salad (See page 30)	Bulgarian Cabernet
Fèta Pecorino	
Palace Bread	Marsala

MIDDLE EASTERN EGG AND VEGETABLE SALAD

Cooking time: 5 minutes
Baking time: 8 minutes

IMPERIAL (METRIC)
2 tablespoonsful olive oil
1 lb (450g) tomatoes, sliced
3 medium-sized green peppers,
  sliced
1 chilli, finely diced
3 cloves garlic, crushed
Sea salt and freshly ground black
  pepper
6-8 eggs

AMERICAN
2 tablespoonsful olive oil
1 lb tomatoes, sliced
3 medium-sized green peppers,
  sliced
1 chili pepper, finely diced
3 cloves garlic, crushed
Sea salt and freshly ground black
  pepper
6-8 eggs

1. Preheat the oven to 350°F/180°C (Gas Mark 4).
2. Heat the oil in a pan and add tomatoes, green peppers, chilli and garlic. Season well and sauté over a low heat until the vegetables are just cooked.
3. Turn the vegetables into a large, shallow earthenware or other baking dish. Break the eggs evenly over the vegetable mixture. Bake for about 8 minutes, or until the eggs are just set. Serve each person one egg with the vegetables underneath.

MOROCCAN POTATO CASSEROLE

Preparation time: 15 minutes
Cooking time: 30 minutes

IMPERIAL (METRIC)
2 lb (900g) potatoes
6 fl oz (180ml) vegetable oil
*3 green peppers, deseeded and
  sliced*
2 teaspoonsful ground cumin
10 cloves garlic, chopped
2 teaspoonful ground coriander
1½ pints (900ml) water
Zest and juice of 1 lemon
*Sea salt and freshly ground black
  pepper*

AMERICAN
2 lb potatoes
¾ cupful vegetable oil
3 green peppers, seeded and sliced
2 teaspoonsful ground cumin
10 cloves garlic, chopped
2 teaspoonsful ground coriander
3¾ cupsful water
Zest and juice of 1 lemon
*Sea salt and freshly ground black
  pepper*

1.   Peel and quarter the potatoes.
2.   Heat the oil in a heavy saucepan. Add the peppers, cumin, garlic and coriander.
3.   Remove from the heat and add the water, lemon zest and juice and potatoes.
4.   Replace the saucepan on the heat and simmer until the potatoes are tender, about 30
     minutes. Season to taste and serve.

OKRA STEW

(Illustrated opposite page 24.)
Cooking time: 35 minutes

IMPERIAL (METRIC)
2 oz (55g) butter
3 onions, sliced
1 lb (450g) okra, tops removed
1 teaspoonful ground coriander
2 tablespoonsful tomato purée
8 fl oz (240ml) water
Juice of 1 lemon
*Sea salt and freshly ground black
  pepper*
Pitta bread to serve

AMERICAN
4 tablespoonsful butter
3 onions, sliced
1 lb okra, tops removed
1 teaspoonful ground coriander
2 tablespoonsful tomato paste
1 cupful water
Juice of 1 lemon
*Sea salt and freshly ground black
  pepper*
Pita bread to serve

1.   Melt the butter in a saucepan. Sauté the onion, then add the okra and coriander and
     continue to cook for 4 minutes.
2.   Add all the remaining ingredients and simmer for 30 minutes. Serve with pitta bread.

COURGETTE RISSOLES

Preparation time: 10 minutes
Cooking time: 20 minutes
Standing time: 30 minutes

IMPERIAL (METRIC)
3 large courgettes
1 tablespoonful flour
2 tablespoonsful chopped parsley
3 oz (85g) curd cheese
1 egg, lightly beaten
Sea salt and freshly ground black
  pepper
Breadcrumbs to coat
2 tablespoonsful oil for frying

AMERICAN
3 large zucchini
1 tablespoonful flour
2 tablespoonsful chopped parsley
⅓ cupful cottage cheese
1 egg, lightly beaten
Sea salt and freshly ground black
  pepper
Bread crumbs to coat
2 tablespoonsful oil for frying

1. Grate the courgettes into a colander and sprinkle with salt. Leave for 30 minutes.
2. Rinse the courgettes under cold water, then squeeze all the moisture out with your hands. Place in a mixing bowl.
3. Add the flour, parsley, cheese, egg and seasoning. Mix well. Mould into golf ball-sized pieces and roll in the breadcrumbs.
4. Heat the oil and shallow-fry the rissoles until they are golden brown. Keep warm in the oven until ready to serve.

PALACE BREAD

Preparation time: 5 minutes
Cooking time: 12 minutes
Cooling time: 1 hour

IMPERIAL (METRIC)
½ lb (225g) honey
½ lb (225g) butter
½ lb (225g) raw cane sugar
4 oz (115g) fresh breadcrumbs
Whipped cream to serve

AMERICAN
⅔ cupful honey
1 cupful (2 sticks) butter
1 cupful raw cane sugar
2 cupsful fresh bread crumbs
Whipped cream to serve

1. Mix honey, butter and sugar together in a saucepan and stir until everything is melted and well-mixed.
2. Pour in the breadcrumbs and cook the mixture over a gentle heat, stirring for 10-12 minutes until a sticky mass is formed.
3. Remove from the heat. Turn out into a 6½ × 3-inch (16 × 7.5cm) soufflé dish.
4. Cool. This dessert can be turned out of the mould and cut like a cake. Serve with whipped cream.

WINTER MENU 10

Leek and Potato Soup   Alsace Sylvaner or Riesling

Cannelloni Stuffed with Spinach and Almonds   Chianti Classico
Cabbage with Bitter Marmalade
Green Salad (See page 30)

Petit-Suisse
Pipo Crem'

Zabaglione   Marsala

LEEK AND POTATO SOUP

Preparation time: 10 minutes
Cooking time: 20 minutes, plus reheating

IMPERIAL (METRIC)	AMERICAN
1 lb (450g) leeks	*1 lb leeks*
½ lb (225g) potatoes	*½ lb potatoes*
2 oz (55g) butter	*4 tablespoonsful butter*
Sea salt and freshly ground black pepper	*Sea salt and freshly ground black pepper*
2 pints (1.2 litres) boiling water	*5 cupsful boiling water*
¼ pint (150ml) single cream	*⅔ cupful light cream*

1. Wash the leeks, cut in half lengthways, then cut into small strips. Peel and dice the potatoes.
2. Melt the butter in a saucepan and sauté the vegetables for a moment. Add salt and pepper and the boiling water.
3. Simmer for 20 minutes, or until the potatoes are soft. Remove from the heat and allow to cool.
4. Blend to a thin purée.
5. Reheat carefully and add the cream at the last moment. Do not let the soup boil. Taste and adjust the seasoning.

CANNELLONI STUFFED WITH SPINACH AND ALMONDS

Preparation time: 10 minutes
Cooking time: 15 minutes
Baking time: 20 minutes

IMPERIAL (METRIC)	AMERICAN
12-16 sheets cannelloni	*12-16 sheets cannelloni*
2 lb (900g) leaf spinach	*2 lb leaf spinach*
2 oz (55g) butter	*4 tablespoonsful butter*
4 oz (115g) ground almonds	*1 cupful ground almonds*
2 tablespoonsful double cream	*2 tablespoonsful heavy cream*
Sea salt and freshly ground black pepper	*Sea salt and freshly ground black pepper*
2 oz (55g) grated gruyère cheese	*½ cupful grated unprocessed gruyère cheese*
½ pint (300ml) single cream	*1¼ cupsful light cream*
2 oz (55g) grated parmesan cheese	*½ cupful grated parmesan cheese*

1. In a large saucepan full of boiling salted water, cook the cannelloni until it is just done, about 10 minutes. Remove from the heat and immediately slip into a bowl of cold water with a little oil in it, so that the cannelloni doesn't stick together.

2. Remove the stalks from the spinach and discard. Cook the spinach leaves in half the butter over a very low heat. The spinach should have shrunk to less than half its bulk and be cooked through in 5-6 minutes. Cool and drain off the excess liquid.

3. Place the spinach in a bowl and chop it up into small pieces with a wooden spoon. Add the almonds, remaining butter, double cream, seasoning and gruyère cheese. Mix well.

4. Drain the cannelloni on kitchen paper. Take one sheet of cannelloni and lay a portion of the spinach mixture on it. Roll up, tucking in the ends. Do the same for the remainder of the cannelloni and stuffing.

5. Preheat the oven to 300°F/150°C (Gas Mark 2). Butter a large, shallow earthenware dish and place the cannelloni in snugly, side by side.

6. Pour the single cream over the cannelloni, then sprinkle the parmesan cheese over the top. Bake for about 20 minutes, until the cannelloni is heated through and the cheese is melted. Serve piping hot.

CABBAGE WITH BITTER MARMALADE

Preparation time: 5 minutes
Cooking time: 7 minutes

IMPERIAL (METRIC)
1 large savoy or white cabbage
2 oz (55g) butter
3 tablespoonsful bitter marmalade
Sea salt and white pepper

AMERICAN
1 large savoy or white cabbage
4 tablespoonsful butter
3 tablespoonsful bitter marmalade
Sea salt and white pepper

1. Slice the cabbage very thinly.
2. Heat the butter in a large saucepan. Throw in the cabbage and season it. Cover the saucepan and simmer for 3-4 minutes.
3. Stir the cabbage well. Add the marmalade and let it cook for another 2 minutes. The cabbage should be *al dente*.
4. Serve immediately or keep hot in a warm oven for a few minutes, but no longer. The cabbage must not be overcooked.

ZABAGLIONE

Preparation time: 5 minutes
Cooking time: 5 minutes

IMPERIAL (METRIC)
6 eggs yolks
3 oz (85g) caster sugar
2½ fl oz (75ml) marsala
Boudoir biscuits to serve

AMERICAN
6 egg yolks
6 tablespoonsful superfine sugar
⅓ cupful marsala
Ladyfingers to serve

1. Place egg yolks and sugar in the top of a double boiler and beat well, add the marsala and beat again. Heat gently, beating all the time, until the mixture is thick and creamy and forms soft peaks.
2. Pour into 6-8 glasses and serve with boudoir biscuits.

WINTER MENU 11

Potage Bonne Femme	Sauvignon
Gourmet Vegetable Pie	Medoc
Cauliflower with Avocado and Tahini Sauce	
Endive and Grapefruit Salad	
Emmental	
Roquefort	
	Calvados or
Ginger Ice Cream	Muscat

POTAGE BONNE FEMME

Preparation time: 5 minutes
Cooking time: 20 minutes, plus reheating

IMPERIAL (METRIC)	AMERICAN
2 oz (55g) butter	4 tablespoonsful butter
1 lettuce heart, chopped	1 lettuce heart, chopped
1 cucumber, chopped	1 cucumber, chopped
2 sprigs fresh tarragon or	2 sprigs fresh tarragon or
1 teaspoonful dried tarragon	1 teaspoonful dried tarragon
2½ pints (1.5 litres) vegetable stock	6 cupsful vegetable stock
Sea salt and freshly ground black pepper	Sea salt and freshly ground black pepper
Pinch of nutmeg	Pinch of nutmeg
2 egg yolks, lightly beaten	2 egg yolks, lightly beaten
½ pint (300ml) single cream	1¼ cupsful light cream
Chopped parsley to garnish	Chopped parsley to garnish

1. Heat the butter in a saucepan and sauté the lettuce and cucumber. Add the tarragon and simmer for several minutes.
2. Add the vegetable stock, seasoning and nutmeg. Continue to simmer for 15 minutes, remove from the heat and leave to cool.
3. Blend to a thin purée.
4. Mix the egg yolks and cream in a bowl. Reheat the soup and pour a little into the egg yolks and cream. Mix well. Pour in a little more of the soup, then stir this mixture back into the soup and reheat gently. Garnish with chopped parsley.

GOURMET VEGETABLE PIE

Preparation time: 20 minutes
Cooking time: 20 minutes
Baking time: 45 minutes

IMPERIAL (METRIC)	AMERICAN
1 aubergine	*1 eggplant*
Flour, beaten egg and breadcrumbs to coat	*Flour, beaten egg and bread crumbs to coat*
Oil for frying	*Oil for frying*
1 lb (450g) tomatoes	*1 lb tomatoes*
10 cloves garlic, crushed	*10 cloves garlic, crushed*
¾ lb (340g) onion, diced	*2 cupsful diced onion*
4 oz (115g) grated gruyère cheese	*1 cupful grated unprocessed gruyère cheese*
½ pint (300ml) single cream	*1¼ cupsful light cream*
1 14-oz (395g) tin artichoke hearts	*1 14-oz can artichoke hearts*
3 oz (85g) grated parmesan cheese	*¾ cupful grated parmesan cheese*
¾ lb (340g) shortcrust pastry	*12 oz shortcrust pastry*

1. Cut the aubergines (eggplants) into 6-8 ½-inch (1.25cm) slices. (Allow 1 slice for each person.) Place the flour, beaten egg and breadcrumbs into separate dishes and dip the aubergine into each dish in that order. Heat the oil in a frying pan and shallow-fry the aubergine until the coating is crisp and brown. Drain and arrange the aubergine in the bottom of a large earthenware dish.
2. Make the sauce. Blanch the tomatoes in boiling water for 30 seconds, then peel. Chop the flesh and cook in 2 tablespoonsful olive oil along with the garlic, until it softens and becomes a purée, about 15 minutes. Remove from the heat and spoon over the aubergine slices.
3. Sprinkle half the onions on top of the sauce and all of the gruyère cheese. Pour half the cream on top.
4. Drain the artichoke hearts well and layer on top of the cream. Sprinkle with the remaining onions and parmesan cheese. Pour the rest of the cream over the top.
5. Preheat the oven to 400°F/200°C (Gas Mark 6).
6. Roll out the pastry to fit over the top of the pie. Brush with beaten egg and bake for 45 minutes or until the crust is brown.

CAULIFLOWER WITH AVOCADO AND TAHINI SAUCE

Preparation time: 10 minutes
Cooking time: 5 minutes

IMPERIAL (METRIC)
1 large cauliflower, separated into
  florets
Juice of 1 lemon
1 large ripe avocado
½ lb (225g) tahini (sesame paste)
Sea salt
2 tablespoonsful toasted sesame
  seeds

AMERICAN
1 large cauliflower, separated into
  florets
Juice of 1 lemon
1 large ripe avocado
½ lb tahini (sesame paste)
Sea salt
2 tablespoonsful toasted sesame
  seeds

1. Boil the cauliflower in salted water and lemon juice for about 3 minutes, just until it is *al dente*. Drain well.
2. Peel and stone the avocado and mash the flesh with the *tahini*. Add salt to taste and mix into a smooth paste.
3. Place the cauliflower into a shallow ovenproof dish, cover with the sauce and sprinkle with the sesame seeds. Before serving, put into a warm oven to heat through for a few minutes.

ENDIVE AND GRAPEFRUIT SALAD

Preparation time: 15 minutes

IMPERIAL (METRIC)
2 grapefruits
1 curly endive
1 teaspoonful raspberry vinegar
Sea salt and white pepper
2 tablespoonsful olive oil

AMERICAN
2 grapefruits
1 chicory
1 teaspoonful raspberry vinegar
Sea salt and white pepper
2 tablespoonsful olive oil

1. Peel the grapefruit, remove all the white pith and pips and cut the flesh into slices. Drink the juice and put the grapefruit into a large salad bowl.
2. Cut the central core off the endive (chicory) and discard. Separate the leaves and toss with the grapefruit.
3. Make the dressing. Add salt and pepper to the vinegar, then add the olive oil. Mix well and pour over the salad.

GINGER ICE CREAM

Cooking time:	25 minutes
Freezing time:	4 hours

IMPERIAL (METRIC)	AMERICAN
1 egg, plus 3 egg yolks	*1 egg, plus 3 egg yolks*
2 tablespoonsful soft brown sugar	*2 tablespoonsful soft brown sugar*
½ pint (300ml) milk	*1¼ cupsful milk*
8-oz (225g) tin preserved ginger	*8-oz can preserved ginger*
½ pint (300ml) double cream, whipped	*1¼ cupsful heavy cream, whipped*

1. Place the eggs and sugar in a bowl and whisk together. Bring the milk to the boil and slowly pour it over the eggs, beating all the time. Pour the mixture back into the pan and cook slowly over a moderate heat until the custard thickens.
2. Place the pan in a bowl of cold water to cool quickly.
3. Drain the preserved ginger, reserving 4 tablespoonsful syrup. Add the syrup to the custard and mix well. Set the ginger aside.
4. Pour the custard into a suitable container and place in the freezer.
5. Measure out 6 oz/170g/1 cupful preserved ginger and chop.
6. When the custard has set around the edges, remove to a bowl and whisk vigorously. Add the ginger and fold in the whipped cream. Return to the freezer for about 2-4 hours.
7. Half an hour before serving, place the ice cream in the refrigerator to soften slightly. Serve in dessert glasses.

WINTER MENU 12

Almond Soup	**Bordeaux Graves Blancs**
Lasagne Verde **Salad Angevine**	**Saint-Emilion**
Cantal **Cheddar**	
Poor Knights of Windsor	**Calvados**

BASIC CELERY STOCK

Preparation time: 10 minutes
Cooking time: 45 minutes

IMPERIAL (METRIC)	AMERICAN
2 heads celery	*2 bunches celery*
2 large onions	*2 large onions*
1 bunch parsley stalks	*1 bunch parsley stalks*
3 pints (1.8 litres) water	*2 quarts water*
Seasoning to taste	*Seasoning to taste*

1. Chop up the vegetables and bring to the boil in the measured water. Simmer for 30 minutes, then cool.
2. Liquidize in an electric blender, then sieve, discarding the remains of the vegetables.
Note: This stock can be made in quantity and then happily be kept in a screw top container in the refrigerator for several weeks.

ALMOND SOUP

Preparation time: 10 minutes
Cooking time: 35 minutes

IMPERIAL (METRIC)	AMERICAN
1 bay leaf	*1 bay leaf*
2½ pints (1.5 litres) celery stock (page 49)	*6 cupsful celery stock (page 49)*
4 oz (115g) ground almonds	*1 cupful ground almonds*
½ pint (300ml) milk	*1¼ cupsful milk*
1 tablespoonful arrowroot	*1 tablespoonful arrowroot*
¼ pint (150ml) double cream	*⅔ cupful heavy cream*
1 tablespoonful butter	*1 tablespoonful butter*
Sea salt and white pepper	*Sea salt and white pepper*
2 oz (55g) toasted or fried almonds to garnish	*⅓ cupful toasted or fried almonds to garnish*

1. Mix the bay leaf, celery stock and almonds together and simmer for 30 minutes. Remove the bay leaf and discard. Add the milk and blend into the soup.
2. Mix the arrowroot with the cream, add to the soup and place over a gentle heat until it thickens. Stir in the butter and add salt and pepper to taste.
3. Pour into a warmed soup tureen and float the almonds on top.

LASAGNE VERDE

Preparation time: 15 minutes
Cooking time: 20 minutes
Baking time: 40 minutes

IMPERIAL (METRIC)	AMERICAN
10-12 sheets lasagne	*10-12 sheets lasagne*
1½ lb (680g) leaf spinach	*1½ lb leaf spinach*
3 oz (85g) butter	*6 tablespoonsful butter*
Sea salt and freshly ground black pepper	*Sea salt and freshly ground black pepper*
1 pint (600ml) single cream	*2½ cupsful light cream*
2 oz (55g) flour	*½ cupful flour*
½ pint (300ml) milk	*1¼ cupsful milk*
8 oz (225g) grated sage derby cheese	*2 cupsful grated vermont sage cheese*
1 oz (30g) fresh breadcrumbs	*½ cupful fresh bread crumbs*
4 oz (115g) grated parmesan cheese	*1 cupful grated parmesan cheese*
1 oz (30g) chopped parsley	*½ cupful chopped parsley*

1. In a saucepan full of boiling salted water, cook the lasagne until it is just done, about 10 minutes. Remove from the heat and immediately slip into a bowl of cold water with a little oil in it, so that the lasagne doesn't stick together.
2. Remove the stalks from the spinach and discard. Cook the spinach leaves in half the butter over a very low heat. The spinach should have shrunk to less than half its bulk and be cooked through in about 5 minutes. Remove from the heat and season with salt

and pepper. Drain off the liquid and reserve for the cheese sauce. Chop the spinach into small pieces with a wooden spoon.

3. Drain the lasagne on kitchen paper. Butter a large shallow earthenware dish. Use half the lasagne to line the bottom and sides of the dish.

4. Strew the spinach evenly over the pasta base and pour over the cream. Layer the rest of the lasagne over the spinach.

5. Make a roux with the flour and remaining butter. Add the spinach liquid, milk and Sage Derby cheese. Season to taste and cook gently until sauce thickens. Remove the sauce from the heat and allow to cool, then pour over the top of the lasagne. Sprinkle the surface with the breadcrumbs, parmesan cheese and parsley.

6. Preheat the oven to 375°F/190°C (Gas Mark 5). Bake the lasagne for 40 minutes or until the top is brown and bubbling.

SALAD ANGEVINE

Preparation time: 10 minutes

IMPERIAL (METRIC)	AMERICAN
1 lb (450g) cooked new potatoes	*1 lb cooked new potatoes*
1 lb (450g) cooked French beans	*1 lb cooked French beans*
3 tablespoonsful walnut oil	*3 tablespoonsful walnut oil*
2 teaspoonsful lemon juice	*2 teaspoonsful lemon juice*
Sea salt and freshly ground black	*Sea salt and freshly ground black*
* pepper*	* pepper*
1 lb (450g) cooked flageolet beans	*1 lb cooked flageolet beans*

1. Cube the potatoes. Cut the French beans into 1-inch (2.5cm) lengths.
2. Mix the walnut oil, lemon juice, salt and pepper together in a large salad bowl.
3. Add the potatoes, flageolet beans and French beans and toss thoroughly.

POOR KNIGHTS OF WINDSOR

Preparation time: 10 minutes
Cooking time: 5 minutes

IMPERIAL (METRIC)	AMERICAN
1 large brioche loaf	*1 large brioche loaf*
4 egg yolks, beaten	*4 egg yolks, beaten*
Butter for frying	*Butter for frying*
2½ fl oz (75ml) sherry	*⅓ cupful sherry*
2 tablespoonsful raw cane sugar	*2 tablespoonsful raw cane sugar*
½ pint (300ml) double cream, whipped	*1¼ cupsful heavy cream, whipped*

1. Cut 6-8 1-inch (2.5cm) slices from the brioche and dip evenly into the egg yolks.
2. Heat the butter in a frying pan and fry the egg-dipped bread until it is crisp and golden on both sides. Remove from the heat and keep warm.
3. Mix the sherry with the sugar and fold into the whipped cream.
4. Serve the brioche slices topped with the flavoured whipped cream.

WINTER MENU 13

Locket's Savoury   Dry Sherry

Caribbean Black Beans   Red Bordeaux
Spinach and Courgette Tart   or Cabernet
Mushrooms à la Grecque

Cheddar
Dolcelatte

Chocolate Peppermint Parfait   Eau de Vie

LOCKET'S SAVOURY

Preparation time: 10 minutes
Baking time: 10-15 minutes

IMPERIAL (METRIC)
6-8 slices wholemeal bread
Butter
1 large bunch watercress
3-4 large ripe pears
6-8 slices Stilton cheese

AMERICAN
6-8 slices wholewheat bread
Butter
1 large bunch watercress
3-4 large ripe pears
6-8 slices Stilton cheese

1. Remove the crusts from the bread, toast lightly, butter, and lay on a baking tray in one layer.
2. Chop the watercress and sprinkle it on top of the toast.
3. Pare the pears and cut in half lengthways. Place each pear half on a slice of toast.
4. Place the cheese slices over the pears.
5. Preheat the oven to 375°F/190°C (Gas Mark 5). Place the baking tray in the oven until the cheese begins to melt, about 10-15 minutes.

CARIBBEAN BLACK BEANS

Soaking time: overnight
Cooking time: 1 ¾ hours

IMPERIAL (METRIC)
¾ lb (340g) dried black beans
3 tablespoonsful olive oil
2 pints (1.2 litres) celery stock (see
*   page 49)*
2 oz (55g) grated root ginger
1 teaspoonful each: freshly ground
*   rosemary, oregano and thyme*
½ teaspoonful chilli powder
2 large onions
1 large parsnip, cubed
Sea salt

AMERICAN
¾ lb dried black beans
3 tablespoonsful olive oil
5 cupsful celery stock (see page 49)
¾ cupful grated root ginger
1 teaspoonful each: freshly ground
*   rosemary, oregano and thyme*
½ teaspoonful chili powder
2 large onions
1 large parsnip, cubed
Sea salt

1. Soak the beans overnight. Drain, boil them in water for 10 minutes, then drain again.
2. Stir the beans into half the olive oil and add the celery stock. Bring to the boil. Simmer for about 1 hour, after which the beans should just be cooked through. Remove from the heat and set aside.
3. In another pan, heat the rest of the oil and sauté the ginger, rosemary, oregano, thyme and chilli powder for a moment, then add the onions and parsnip. Add enough water to cover and simmer for 10 minutes.
4. Add the beans to the vegetables and continue to cook for another 20 minutes. (They may need a little more water.) The beans should now be done if they have soaked up all the liquid and flavours. Taste and add salt as necessary.

SPINACH AND COURGETTE TART

Preparation time: 10 minutes
Baking time: 55 minutes
Cooking time: 10 minutes
Standing time: 10-15 minutes

IMPERIAL (METRIC)	AMERICAN
¾ lb (340g) shortcrust pastry	*12 oz shortcrust pastry*

Filling:

2 lb (900g) leaf spinach	*2 lb leaf spinach*
1 oz (30g) butter	*2 tablespoonsful butter*
1 lb (450g) courgettes, sliced	*1 lb zucchini, sliced*
5 eggs	*5 eggs*
½ pint (300ml) single cream	*1¼ cupsful light cream*
Sea salt and freshly ground black pepper	*Sea salt and freshly ground black pepper*
4 oz (115g) curd cheese	*½ cupful curd cheese*
2 oz (55g) grated gruyère cheese	*½ cupful grated unprocessed gruyère cheese*
2 oz (55g) grated parmesan cheese	*½ cupful grated parmesan cheese*

1. Line a 11-12-inch (27.5-30cm) pie or flan tin with the shortcrust pastry and bake blind in a preheated oven (400°F/200°C/Gas Mark 6) for 10 minutes. Remove from the oven and allow to cool. Reduce the oven temperature to 375°F/190°C (Gas Mark 5).
2. Remove the spinach stalks and discard. Cook the spinach leaves in the butter for 10 minutes. Drain off the liquid and reserve.
3. In the meantime, cook the courgettes (zucchini) in a little salted water for about 10 minutes. Drain.
4. Mix the courgettes with the spinach in a large bowl. In another bowl, beat the eggs with the cream, reserved spinach liquid, salt and pepper.
5. Break up the curd cheese and mix into the spinach and courgettes. Add the egg-cream mixture. Combine all the ingredients well, then pour into the pie dish. Sprinkle the top with the grated gruyère and parmesan cheese.
6. Place the tart in the top half of the oven and bake for 40-45 minutes, or until the top has risen and is golden brown. Let the tart rest for about 10-15 minutes before being cut. It should be eaten warm.

MUSHROOMS À LA GRECQUE

Preparation time: 10 minutes
Cooking time: 10 minutes

IMPERIAL (METRIC)
1 lb (450g) mushrooms
3 tablespoonsful olive oil
2 bay leaves
2 teaspoonsful crushed coriander
  seeds
Sea salt and freshly ground black
  pepper
Juice of 1 lemon

AMERICAN
1 lb mushrooms
3 tablespoonsful olive oil
2 bay leaves
2 teaspoonsful crushed coriander
  seeds
Sea salt and freshly ground black
  pepper
Juice of 1 lemon

1. Wash the mushrooms and pat dry (never peel them). Slice thinly.
2. Heat the oil in a large frying pan. Add the bay leaves and crushed coriander, sauté for a moment, then add the mushrooms. Cook over a gentle heat for about 10 minutes.
3. Remove from the heat. Discard the bay leaves. Season with salt and pepper, pour the lemon juice over and place in a serving dish.

CHOCOLATE PEPPERMINT PARFAIT

Preparation time: 5 minutes
Cooking time: 5 minutes
Cooling time: 30 minutes
Freezing time: 2-4 hours

IMPERIAL (METRIC)
1 oz (30g) raw cane sugar
¼ pint (150ml) water
½ lb (225g) chocolate peppermint
  creams
4 egg yolks
¼ pint (150ml) double cream
1 tablespoonful crème de menthe

AMERICAN
2 tablespoonsful raw cane sugar
⅔ cupful water
½ lb chocolate peppermint creams
4 egg yolks
⅔ cupful heavy cream
1 tablespoonful crème de menthe

1. Boil the sugar and water together in a heavy saucepan for 3 minutes.
2. Pour the sugar syrup into a blender container. Add the chocolate peppermint creams and blend until smooth. Add the egg yolks and blend again. Leave to cool for about 30 minutes.
3. Blend the cream and liqueur into the chocolate-peppermint mixture. Pour into 6-8 ramekin dishes and place in the freezer for 2-4 hours. Serve straight from the freezer.

SPRING MENUS

SPRING MENU 1

Fresh Asparagus with Butter and Lemon Sauce	Pinot Bianco
Oeufs Florentine	Côtes-du-Rhône
Piyazi	
New Potatoes with Mint	
Salade de Pissenlits	
Triple-Crème Frais	
Saint-Paulin	
Emmental	
Rhubarb Fool	Sauternes

FRESH ASPARAGUS WITH BUTTER AND LEMON SAUCE

Preparation time: 10 minutes
Cooking time: 12 minutes

IMPERIAL (METRIC)
36-48 thick asparagus stalks or *one dozen thin ones per person*

Sauce:
½ lb (225g) slightly salted butter
8 tablespoonsful fresh lemon juice
Sea salt and freshly ground black pepper

AMERICAN
36-48 thick asparagus stalks or *one dozen thin ones per person*

1 cupful (2 sticks) slightly salted butter
½ cupful fresh lemon juice
Sea salt and freshly ground black pepper

1. Cook the asparagus. Cooking time depends upon the thickness of the spears. Simmer thick ones for 8 minutes or steam for 10 minutes.(Thin ones will be done in about 5 minutes.) Keep warm.
2. Melt the butter in a saucepan, let it froth, then add the lemon juice bit by bit, stirring all the time. Season with a pinch of salt and pepper to taste and pour into a sauceboat.

OEUFS FLORENTINE

Preparation time: 5 minutes
Cooking time: 12 minutes
Baking time: 15 minutes

IMPERIAL (METRIC)
2 lb (900g) leaf spinach
2 oz (55g) butter
6-8 eggs
1 oz (30g) plain flour
½ pint (300ml) milk
4 oz (115g) grated gruyère cheese
4 oz (115g) grated cheddar cheese
Sea salt and freshly ground black
*   pepper*

AMERICAN
2 lb leaf spinach
4 tablespoonsful butter
6-8 eggs
¼ cupful flour
1¼ cupsful milk
1 cupful grated unprocessed gruyère
*   cheese*
1 cupful grated cheddar cheese
Sea salt and freshly ground black
*   pepper*

1.   Tear the stalks from the spinach and discard. Cook the spinach leaves with half the butter over a low heat for 5-7 minutes, or until they are soft.
2.   With a wooden spoon, chop the leaves finely. Drain the liquor and reserve.
3.   In a large, flat earthenware dish, spread out the spinach. Make 6-8 hollows with the back of a spoon and break an egg into each hollow.
4.   Make a roux with the rest of the butter and the flour. Add the spinach liquor, milk, cheese and seasoning to taste. Cook until the sauce thickens.
5.   Pour the sauce over the eggs and spinach, place in a preheated oven 350°F/180°C (Gas Mark 4) and bake for 15 minutes.

PIYAZI (Turkish Pepper Salad)

Soaking time: overnight
Preparation time: 10 minutes
Cooking time: 1¼ hours

IMPERIAL (METRIC)
10 oz (285g) dried haricot beans
2 green peppers
2 red peppers
4 large tomatoes
2 tablespoonsful olive oil
2 tablespoonsful lemon juice
Sea salt and freshly ground black
*   pepper*
12 stoned black olives
Bunch of parsley

AMERICAN
1⅓ cupsful dried navy beans
2 green peppers
2 red peppers
4 large tomatoes
2 tablespoonsful olive oil
2 tablespoonsful lemon juice
Sea salt and freshly ground black
*   pepper*
12 pitted black olives
Bunch of parsley

1.   Soak beans overnight.
2.   Cook the beans in plenty of boiling water for 1¼ hours or until they are tender. Drain.
3.   Slice the peppers thinly and discard the seeds and pith. Slice the tomatoes.

4. Heat the oil in a shallow pan and cook peppers and tomatoes for 1 minute. Add the beans and lemon juice, give everything a good stir and season to taste. Make sure everything is hot.
5. Pour into a dish, decorate with the olives and parsley and serve immediately.

Note: The peppers and tomatoes do not have to be cooked. They should be hot, but almost raw.

NEW POTATOES WITH MINT

Preparation time: 5 minutes
Cooking time: 20 minutes

IMPERIAL (METRIC)	AMERICAN
2 lb (900g) new potatoes	*2 lb new potatoes*
Fresh mint, chopped	*Fresh mint, chopped*
Melted butter	*Melted butter*

1. Scrub the potatoes skins.
2. Boil the potatoes until they are just done, about 15-20 minutes. Drain and toss them in plenty of chopped mint and melted butter.

SALADE DE PISSENLITS (Dandelion Salad)

Preparation time: 10 minutes

IMPERIAL (METRIC)	AMERICAN
Good-sized bunch of dandelion leaves	*Good-sized bunch of dandelion leaves*
2-3 crisp lettuce hearts	*2-3 crisp lettuce hearts*
2 tablespoonsful walnut oil	*2 tablespoonsful walnut oil*
1 teaspoonful wine vinegar	*1 teaspoonful wine vinegar*
Sea salt and freshly ground black pepper	*Sea salt and freshly ground black pepper*

1. Tear the dandelion leaves into small pieces, quarter the lettuce hearts and place in a large bowl. Add the oil, vinegar and seasoning and mix well.

RHUBARB FOOL

Preparation time: 10 minutes
Cooking time: 10 minutes

IMPERIAL (METRIC)	AMERICAN
2 lb (900g) rhubarb	*2 lb rhubarb*
2 tablespoonsful honey	*2 tablespoonsful honey*
½ pint (300ml) double cream, whipped	*1¼ cupsful heavy cream, whipped*

1. Trim and cut rhubarb into chunks. Cook over a low heat with the honey for at least 10 minutes, or until tender. *Add no liquid at all.* Remove from the heat and let cool.
2. Purée the rhubarb mixture in a blender. Add the whipped cream, mix well and pour into individual glasses.

SPRING MENU 2

(Illustrated between pages 72 and 73.)

Cream of Asparagus Soup	*Chardonnay*
Blinchiki	*Margaux*
Broad Beans	
Artichoke and Potato Salad	
Cantal or Fourme de Rochefort	
Belval	
Sage Lancashire	
Tarte au Citron	*Marc*

CREAM OF ASPARAGUS SOUP

Preparation time: 10 minutes
Cooking time: 10 minutes

IMPERIAL (METRIC)	AMERICAN
2 bunches asparagus	*2 bunches asparagus*
2 pints (1.2 litres) water	*5 cupsful water*
3 oz (85g) butter	*6 tablespoonsful water*
3 oz (85g) onion, chopped	*½ cupful chopped onion*
2 cloves garlic, crushed	*2 cloves garlic, crushed*
1 tablespoonful flour	*1 tablespoonful flour*
Sea salt and freshly ground black pepper	*Sea salt and freshly ground black pepper*
½ pint (300ml) double cream	*1¼ cupsful heavy cream*
Chopped parsley to garnish	*Chopped parsley to garnish*

1. Cut off the tips of the asparagus and boil them in the water until tender. Remove the asparagus tips with a slotted spoon and reserve.
2. Cook the rest of the asparagus in the same water until tender. Leave to cool.
3. Purée the asparagus stalk mixture in a blender. Sieve the mixture and discard any fibrous pieces.
4. Melt the butter in a saucepan, add the onion and garlic and cook until soft. Add the flour and continue to cook over a low heat. Add the asparagus stock and season to taste.
5. Pour the cream into a bowl, add a little of the hot soup and mix well, then pour back into the saucepan and reheat gently. Add the reserved asparagus tips and continue to stir.
6. Before serving, sprinkle the parsley on top.

BLINCHIKI (Pancakes with Carrot Filling)

Preparation time: 5 minutes
Standing time: 1 hour
Cooking time: 45 minutes

IMPERIAL (METRIC)
Pancake batter:
½ lb (225g) plain flour
¼ teaspoonful sea salt
3 eggs
¾ pint milk (450ml) milk
2 tablespoonsful melted butter

Filling:
2 lb (900g) carrots, diced
¾ pint (450ml) water
3 heaped tablespoonsful butter
Pinch of sea salt, freshly ground
  black pepper and sugar
4 hard-boiled eggs, crumbled

AMERICAN

2 cupsful all-purpose flour
¼ teaspoonful sea salt
3 eggs
2 cupsful milk
2 tablespoonsful melted butter

2 lb carrots, diced
2 cupsful water
3 heaping tablespoonsful butter
Pinch of sea salt, freshly ground
  black pepper and sugar
4 hard-cooked eggs, crumbled

1. First make the pancake batter. Sift the flour and salt into a bowl, whisk the eggs with the milk and melted butter and stir into the flour. Leave to rest for 1 hour.
2. Boil the carrots until tender, then drain. Mash together with the butter, seasoning and eggs.
3. Make 12-16 small pancakes or 6-8 larger ones.
4. Place some of the carrot filling in the centre of each pancake and fold over each side like an envelope. Lay the pancakes in a buttered ovenproof dish, dot with a bit more butter and place in a preheated oven 375°F/190°C (Gas Mark 5) for 15 minutes. Serve hot.

BROAD BEANS

Preparation time: 5 minutes
Cooking time: 10 minutes

IMPERIAL (METRIC)
2½ lb (1.1kg) unshelled broad
  beans
Summer savory or *tarragon*
2 tablespoonsful butter or *soured*
  cream

AMERICAN
2½ lb unshelled fava beans
Summer savory or *tarragon*
2 tablespoonsful butter or *sour*
  cream

1. Shell the beans and boil with a little summer savory or tarragon until just tender, about 10 minutes.
2. Toss either in a little butter or soured cream before serving.

ARTICHOKE AND POTATO SALAD

Preparation time: 15 minutes
Cooking time: 20 minutes

IMPERIAL (METRIC)	AMERICAN
2 tablespoonsful walnut oil	*2 tablespoonsful walnut oil*
2 teaspoonsful wine vinegar	*2 teaspoonsful wine vinegar*
Sea salt and freshly ground black pepper	*Sea salt and freshly ground black pepper*
2 lb (900g) new potatoes	*2 lb new potatoes*
1 14-oz (395g) tin artichoke bottoms	*1 14-oz can artichoke bottoms*
3 tablespoonsful chopped fresh mint	*3 tablespoonsful chopped fresh mint*
12 stoned black olives	*12 pitted black olives*

1. Mix the oil, vinegar and seasoning together in a large bowl.
2. Cook the potatoes until tender and drain well. Drain the artichoke bottoms.
3. Dice the potatoes and artichokes, add to the vinaigrette and toss well.
4. Garnish with the mint and olives.

TARTE AU CITRON (Lemon Tart)

Preparation time: 15 minutes
Chilling time: 1 hour
Baking time: 45 minutes

IMPERIAL (METRIC)	AMERICAN
Pastry:	
½ lb (225g) plain flour	*2 cupsful all-purpose flour*
4 egg yolks	*4 egg yolks*
½ teaspoonful salt	*½ teaspoonful salt*
3½ oz (100g) caster sugar	*½ cupful superfine sugar*
½ teaspoonful vanilla essence	*½ teaspoonful vanilla extract*
4 oz (115g) butter	*½ cupful (1 stick) butter*
Lemon Filling:	
2 eggs	*2 eggs*
3½ oz (100g) caster sugar	*½ cupful superfine sugar*
Zest and juice of 1½ lemons	*Zest and juice of 1½ lemons*
4 oz (115g) butter, melted	*½ cup melted butter*
2 oz (55g) whole blanched almonds	*⅓ cupful whole blanched almonds*

1. Make the pastry, wrap in clingfilm and refrigerate for 1 hour.
2. Preheat the oven to 375°F/190°C (Gas Mark 5).
3. Roll out the pastry to fit a 11-12-inch (27.5-30cm) pie dish.
4. Bake the pastry shell blind in the preheated oven for 12-15 minutes or until the pastry is set, but not brown. Remove from the oven.
5. Make the filling. Beat the eggs with the sugar, stir in the lemon zest and juice, then the melted butter and almonds. Pour the filling into the pie shell.
6. Place the baking sheet in the oven to heat. Position the tart on the sheet and bake for 25-30 minutes until the filling is set and golden brown. Serve at room temperature.

SPRING MENU 3

Globe Artichokes   Mâcon Blanc

Blanquette de Pommes de Terre aux Poireaux   Gevrey-
Chou Farci à la Limousine   Chambertin
Watercress and Orange Salad

Coulommiers
Bleu de Gex
Swaledale

Chicolle

GLOBE ARTICHOKES

Preparation time:	5 minutes
Cooking time:	45 minutes

IMPERIAL (METRIC)	AMERICAN
6-8 globe artichokes	*6-8 globe artichokes*
Garlic vinaigrette	*Garlic vinaigrette*

1. Allow 1 artichoke per person. Depending on size, they will take up to 45 minutes to cook in boiling water. Drain well. Make a strong garlic vinaigrette and let the guests pour the sauce over the artichokes at the table.

BLANQUETTE DE POMMES DE TERRE AUX POIREAUX
(White Potato and Leek Stew)
Preparation time:　　10 minutes
Cooking time:　　　25 minutes

IMPERIAL (METRIC)	AMERICAN
2 lb (900g) potatoes	*2 lb potatoes*
1 lb (450g) leeks	*1 lb leeks*
2 oz (55g) butter	*4 tablespoonsful butter*
1 tablespoonful flour	*1 tablespoonful flour*
23 fl oz (690ml) milk	*3 cupsful milk*
Sea salt and freshly ground black pepper	*Sea salt and freshly ground black pepper*
Pinch of nutmeg	*Pinch of nutmeg*
Bouquet garni	*Bouquet garni*

1. Slice the potatoes thinly. Trim the leeks, split in half and slice.
2. Melt the butter in a large, thick-bottomed pan and throw in the leeks. Cook over a low heat until they are soft, about 5 minutes.
3. Sprinkle the flour over the leeks and continue to cook, stirring, for 1 minute.
4. Add the milk and bring to the boil, stirring all the time, to get a smooth sauce. Season and add the potatoes and bouquet garni.
5. Cover the pan and cook over a low heat until the potatoes are falling apart, 15-20 minutes. Taste and adjust seasoning. Pour into a flameproof dish and brown the top under a hot grill.

CHOU FARCE À LA LIMOUSINE (Stuffed Cabbage)
Soaking time:　　　overnight
Preparation time:　　10 minutes
Cooking time:　　　1½ hours

IMPERIAL (METRIC)	AMERICAN
36 cabbage leaves	*36 cabbage leaves*
¾ lb (340g) dried chestnuts	*2 cupsful dried chestnuts*
8 oz (225g) grated strong cheddar cheese	*2 cupsful grated strong cheddar cheese*
Sea salt and freshly ground black pepper	*Sea salt and freshly ground black pepper*
1 teaspoonful ground coriander	*1 teaspoonful ground coriander*
4 oz (115g) butter	*½ cupful (1 stick) butter*

1. Soak chestnuts overnight in water. Drain, then cook in boiling water for 1 hour or more, until they are tender and break up with the point of a knife. Drain well.
2. Blanch the cabbage leaves in boiling water for a few minutes, then drain and pat dry.
3. Pour the chestnuts into a large bowl. Add the cheddar cheese, salt, pepper and coriander. Mix well.
4. Place a spoonful of the chestnut mixture in the centre of each cabbage leaf and roll up, tucking in the ends.

5. Place the cabbage rolls in a large pan so that they fit together snugly. Pour enough water in the pan to come within ½ inch (1.25cm) of the tops of the rolls. Dot with butter. Bring to the boil, cover and simmer for 25 minutes. Remove the lid and continue cooking until the liquid reduces to very little. Serve the cabbage rolls with the cooking liquor poured over them.

WATERCRESS AND ORANGE SALAD
(Illustrated opposite page 72.)
Preparation time: 10 minutes

IMPERIAL (METRIC)	AMERICAN
2-3 oranges	*2-3 oranges*
2-3 bunches watercress	*2-3 bunches watercress*
12 stoned black olives	*12 pitted black olives*
2 tablespoonsful olive oil	*2 tablespoonsful olive oil*
2 teaspoonsful raspberry vinegar	*2 teaspoonsful raspberry vinegar*
Sea salt and freshly ground black pepper	*Sea salt and freshly ground black pepper*

1. Peel and slice the oranges. Cut each slice in half.
2. Wash and trim watercress.
3. Pile the olives in the centre of a large platter. Surround with the orange slices, then arrange the watercress around the outside edge.
4. Mix the oil, vinegar and seasoning and pour over the oranges.

CHICOLLE (Peaches in Red Wine)
Marinating time: 2-3 days
Preparation time: 10 minutes

IMPERIAL (METRIC)	AMERICAN
6-8 ripe peaches	*6-8 ripe peaches*
3½ oz (100g) caster sugar	*½ cupful superfine sugar*
¾ pint (450ml) water	*2 cupsful water*
1 pint (600ml) dry red wine	*2½ cupsful dry red wine*
6-8 slices toasted brioche to serve	*6-8 slices toasted brioche to serve*

1. Peel the peaches 2-3 days in advance of serving. Remove stones, cut into quarters, place into a dish and sprinkle with the sugar. Pour over the water and wine and cover the dish with a plate to prevent the peaches from floating. Refrigerate for 2-3 days.
2. Serve peaches in individual bowls in the marinade, accompanied by toasted brioche, which can be dipped in the wine.

SPRING MENU 4

Broad Bean Soup	Pouilly-Fuissé
Cheese-Stuffed Artichokes	Crozes-
Leek Soufflé	Hermitage
New Potatoes with Mint (See page 61)	
Spinach and Avocado Salad	
Rollot	
Saint-Maure	
Cheddar	
Coupe de Ruffey	

BROAD BEAN SOUP

Cooking time: 15 minutes, plus reheating
Preparation time: 10 minutes

IMPERIAL (METRIC)	AMERICAN
2 oz (55g) butter	*4 tablespoonsful butter*
4 oz (115g) chopped onions	*2/3 cupful chopped onions*
2 cloves garlic, crushed	*2 cloves garlic, crushed*
1¾ pints (1 litre) boiling water	*4 cupsful boiling water*
1 lb (450g) young broad beans, shelled	*1 lb fava beans, shelled*
6 bean pods, trimmed	*6 bean pods, trimmed*
1 tablespoonful chopped fresh sage	*1 tablespoonful chopped fresh sage*
Sea salt and freshly ground black pepper	*Sea salt and freshly ground black pepper*
Pinch of sugar	*Pinch of sugar*
6 tablespoonsful double cream	*6 tablespoonsful heavy cream*
1 teaspoonful lemon juice	*1 teaspoonful lemon juice*
2-3 chopped spring onions	*2-3 chopped scallions*

1. Heat the butter in a saucepan, add the onion and garlic and sauté until soft.
2. Add the beans, boiling water and bean pods. Boil for 10 minutes, or until beans are tender. (Young beans will not need peeling. If older ones are used, take out a few and skin for garnishing.)
3. Blend the soup to a purée, then sieve. Add the sage, seasoning, sugar and cream. Reheat, taste and adjust seasoning, add the lemon juice and finally the spring onions (scallions).

CHEESE-STUFFED ARTICHOKES

(Illustrated opposite page 72.)

Cooking time: 45 minutes
Preparation time: 10 minutes
Baking time: 15 minutes

IMPERIAL (METRIC)	AMERICAN
6-8 globe artichokes	*6-8 globe artichokes*
Butter for greasing	*Butter for greasing*
¾ lb (340g) fromage frais or Quark	*¾ lb fromage frais or low-fat cheese*
3 tablespoonsful capers	*3 tablespoonsful capers*
1 tablespoonful paprika	*1 tablespoonful paprika*
Sea salt and freshly ground black pepper	*Sea salt and freshly ground black pepper*

1. Boil the artichokes until tender, about 45 minutes. Let them cool, then cut out the centre leaves and choke. Scrape any edible flesh from these leaves and reserve in a bowl. Discard the choke and leaves.
2. Butter a flat earthenware dish and place the artichokes into it. Preheat the oven to 450°F/230°C (Gas Mark 8).
3. Add the cheese to the artichoke flesh with the capers, paprika and seasoning. Stuff the artichokes with the mixture and place in the oven for 15 minutes.

LEEK SOUFFLÉ

Cooking time: 10 minutes
Preparation time: 5 minutes
Baking time: 20 minutes

IMPERIAL (METRIC)	AMERICAN
2 oz (55g) butter	*4 tablespoonsful butter*
1 lb (450g) leeks	*1 lb leeks*
1 oz (30g) flour	*¼ cupful flour*
½ pint (300ml) milk	*1¼ cupsful milk*
2 oz (55g) grated parmesan cheese	*½ cupful grated parmesan cheese*
2 oz (55g) grated gruyère cheese	*½ cupful grated gruyère cheese*
½ pint (300ml) single cream	*1¼ cupsful light cream*
Sea salt and freshly ground black pepper	*Sea salt and freshly ground black pepper*
6 eggs, separated	*6 eggs, separated*

1. Heavily butter a 10-inch (25cm) soufflé dish. Cut the leeks in half lengthways, then slice. Cook the leeks over a low heat with 1 tablespoonful butter in a covered pan until tender, about 5 minutes.
2. Melt the remaining butter in another saucepan, make a roux with the flour, then add the milk and cheese and cook gently until the sauce is thickened. Remove from the heat and leave to cool.
3. Pour the leeks and cheese sauce into a large mixing bowl, mix well, then add the cream, seasoning and egg yolks.
4. Preheat the oven to 450°F/230°C (Gas Mark 8).
5. Whisk the egg whites until stiff. Fold them into the leek mixture, ensuring that lots of air is whipped in. Pour into the soufflé dish.
6. Bake for 20 minutes. By then, the souffle should have risen; the inside centre should still be runny. Serve at once.

SPINACH AND AVOCADO SALAD

Preparation time: 10 minutes

IMPERIAL (METRIC)	AMERICAN
1 lb (450g) very young leaf spinach	*1 lb very young leaf spinach*
2 ripe avocados	*2 ripe avocados*
2 tablespoonsful hazelnut oil	*2 tablespoonsful hazelnut oil*
2 teaspoonsful wine vinegar	*2 teaspoonsful wine vinegar*
Sea salt and freshly ground black pepper	*Sea salt and freshly ground black pepper*
3 oz (85g) coarsely chopped hazelnuts	*¾ cupful coarsely chopped hazelnuts (filberts)*

1. Remove the spinach leaves from the stalks, discard the stalks, wash the leaves and pat dry.
2. Peel, stone and slice the avocados.
3. Mix the oil, vinegar and seasoning in a large bowl. Add the avocados and spinach and sprinkle with the hazelnuts.
4. Toss the salad gently at the table, making sure the avocado is well distributed.

COUPE DE RUFFEY (Blackcurrant Sorbet with Grapes)

Marinating time: 1 day
Preparation time: Making the sorbet, plus 5 minutes

IMPERIAL (METRIC)
2 lb (900g) black grapes
¼ pint (150ml) crème de cassis
2½ fl oz (75ml) marc
1¼ pints (.75 litres) blackcurrant
   sorbet, homemade or bought

AMERICAN
2 lb black grapes
⅔ cupful crème de cassis
⅓ cupful marc
3 cupsful black currant sherbert,
   homemade or bought

Sorbet:
1 lb (450g) blackcurrants
½ lb (225g) raw cane sugar
½ pint (300ml) water
Zest and juice of 1 lemon

1 lb black currants or blackberries
1 cupful raw cane sugar
1¼ cupsful water
Zest and juice of 1 lemon

1. If you are making your own sorbet, do this first. Mix all the ingredients together in a saucepan and bring to the boil. Simmer for 5 minutes, remove from the heat, then cool.
2. Blend the blackcurrant mixture to a purée, then sieve. Place the syrup in a suitable container in the freezer. After 1 hour, the mixture should be stiff; stir well to break up the ice crystals, replace in the freezer and repeat the process 1 hour later. Freeze overnight before using.
3. Prepare the grapes. Peel by blanching in boiling water. Remove the pips, then marinate in the crème de cassis and marc for a day. Chill.
4. Just before serving, place a scoop of sorbet in each dessert glass, and spoon over the grapes and liquor.

SPRING MENU 5

Spinach Pâté	White Burgundy
Asparagus Timbale	Saint-Emilion
Artichokes Clamart	
New Potatoes with Mint (See page 61)	
Green Salad (See page 30)	
Brie de Meaux	
Bondon de Neufchatel	
Bleu des Causses	
	Calvados
Clafoutis Limousin	or Marc

SPINACH PÂTÉ

Preparation time:	5 minutes
Cooking time:	5 minutes
Chilling time:	Several hours

IMPERIAL (METRIC)
1 lb (450g) leaf spinach
3 oz (85g) butter
1 bunch spring onions, chopped
Sea salt and freshly ground black
   pepper
5 oz (140g) fromage frais or Quark
Juice of 1 lemon
Wholemeal toast to serve

AMERICAN
1 lb leaf spinach
6 tablespoonsful butter
1 bunch scallions, chopped
Sea salt and freshly ground black
   pepper
2/3 cupful fromage frais or low-fat
   cheese
Juice of 1 lemon
Wholewheat toast to serve

1. Remove the spinach leaves from the stalks, discard the stalks and tear the leaves into small pieces.
2. Melt 2 tablespoonsful butter in a pan and cook the spinach and spring onions (scallions) for about 5 minutes. Leave to cool, then season to taste.
3. Purée the vegetables in a blender, adding the rest of the butter, cheese and lemon juice.
4. Pour the mixture into 6-8 ramekin dishes and refrigerate until set.
5. Serve with wholemeal toast.

Opposite: Cheese Stuffed Artichokes (page 69) *and* Watercress Orange Salad (page 67).
Overleaf: Spring Menu 2 (pages 62 to 64).

ASPARAGUS TIMBALE

Preparation time: 15 minutes
Cooking time: 15 minutes
Baking time: 45 minutes

IMPERIAL (METRIC)
1 bunch asparagus
½ pint (300ml) milk
3 tablespoonsful butter
2 oz (55g) breadcrumbs
1 oz (30g) finely chopped onion
2 oz (55g) grated cheddar cheese
Sea salt and freshly ground black
   pepper
Pinch of nutmeg

AMERICAN
1 bunch asparagus
1¼ cupsful milk
3 tablspoonsful butter
½ cupful breadcrumbs
¼ cupful minced onion
½ cupful grated cheddar cheese
Sea salt and freshly ground black
   pepper
Pinch of nutmeg

1. Trim the asparagus and chop into small pieces. Simmer in the milk until soft. Remove 5-6 tips for garnishing and reserve. Purée the remainder of the asparagus and milk, then sieve. Set aside.
2. Grease a 6½ × 3-inch (16 × 7.5cm) soufflé dish with 1 tablespoonful of the butter. Press the breadcrumbs onto the bottom and sides of the dish. Preheat the oven to 350°F/180°C (Gas Mark 4).
3. Cook the onion in the remaining butter until soft. Put into a mixing bowl and add the cheese, seasoning and nutmeg.
4. Break the eggs into the bowl and whisk well.
5. Heat the asparagus stock and slowly add it to the egg and cheese mixture, stirring all the time. Pour the mixture into the prepared mould and place in a *bain marie* in the oven.
6. Bake for about 45 minutes. The custard is done when a knife inserted in the centre comes out clean. Let the custard settle for 5 minutes before removing it from the oven.
7. Invert the mould over a warm platter and the timbale should come out easily. Decorate the top with the reserved asparagus tips.

Opposite: Clafoutis Limousin (page 75).

ARTICHOKES CLAMART

Cooking time: 30 minutes
Preparation time: 5 minutes

IMPERIAL (METRIC)	AMERICAN
Leaves of 1 small lettuce	*Leaves of 1 small lettuce*
1 bunch spring onions, chopped	*1 bunch scallions, chopped*
1 lb (450g) shelled peas	*1 lb shelled peas*
2 young carrots, diced	*2 young carrots, diced*
3 tablespoonsful chopped parsley	*3 tablspoonsful chopped parsley*
¼ teaspoonful sea salt	*¼ teaspoonful sea salt*
3 tablespoonsful butter	*3 tablespoonsful butter*
4 tablespoonsful water	*4 tablespoonsful water*
6-8 tinned artichokes bottoms	*6-8 tinned artichokes bottoms*

1. Place the lettuce leaves in the base of a thick-bottomed saucepan. Add all the remaining ingredients except the artichokes and 1 tablespoonful of the parsley. Cook over a low heat for 20-30 minutes.
2. Butter a flat earthenware dish, lay the artichoke bottoms in the dish and heat in the oven.
3. When the vegetables are done, spoon them over the artichokes and sprinkle with the remaining parsley.

CLAFOUTIS LIMOUSIN (Cherry Bake)

(Illustrated opposite page 73.)
Preparation time: 15 minutes
Baking time: 45 minutes

IMPERIAL (METRIC)
1 lb (450g) small, black tart cherries
1 oz (30g) flour
Pinch of sea salt
2 oz (55g) caster sugar
4 eggs
1 pint (600ml) milk
2 egg yolks
4 tablespoonsful cognac
Icing sugar

AMERICAN
1 lb small, black tart cherries
¼ cupful flour
Pinch of sea salt
¼ cupful superfine sugar
4 eggs
2½ cupsful milk
2 egg yolks
4 tablespoonsful cognac
Confectioner's sugar

1. Butter a shallow baking dish. Preheat the oven to 375°F/190°C (Gas Mark 5).
2. Stone the cherries and lay them in the buttered dish.
3. Make the batter. Sift the flour, salt and sugar into a bowl. Beat in the whole eggs, two at a time, alternating with the milk. Beat in the egg yolks and pour the batter over the cherries. Spoon the cognac on top.
4. Bake for 45 minutes or until the *clafoutis* is puffed and brown.
5. Sprinkle with the icing sugar and serve warm.

```
┌─────────────────────────────────────────────────────────┐
│                                                          │
│              SPRING MENU 6                               │
│                                                          │
│  Cauliflower Fritters with Sesame Sauce        Soave    │
│                                                          │
│  Green Pea Tart                                Côte de  │
│  Artichokes à la Polita                        Brouilly │
│  Catalan Spinach                                        │
│  Crisp Lettuce Salad                                    │
│                                                          │
│  Coeur d'Arras                                          │
│  Pithiviers au Foin                                     │
│                                                          │
│  Pesche Ripiene                                Sauternes│
│                                                          │
└─────────────────────────────────────────────────────────┘
```

CAULIFLOWER FRITTERS WITH SESAME SAUCE

Preparation time: 10 minutes
Standing time: 2 hours
Cooking time: 10-15 minutes

IMPERIAL (METRIC)	AMERICAN
Batter:	
4 oz (115g) plain or gram flour	1 cupful all-purpose or chick pea flour
½ teaspoonful sea salt	½ teaspoonful sea salt
2 tablespoonsful corn oil	2 tablespoonsful corn oil
6 fl oz (180ml) water	¾ cupful water
1 egg white	1 egg white
Sauce:	
3 tablespoonsful tahini (sesame paste)	3 tablespoonsful tahini (sesame paste)
2 tablespoonsful lemon juice	2 tablespoonsful lemon juice
3 tablespoonsful water	3 tablespoonsful water
Drop of tabasco sauce	Drop of tabasco sauce
½ teaspoonful sea salt	½ teaspoonful sea salt
1 large cauliflower, cut into florets	1 large cauliflower, cut into florets
Oil for frying	Oil for frying
3-4 lemons, cut in half to serve	3-4 lemons, cut in half to serve

1. Make the batter. Sift the flour and salt together, add the oil, stir and gradually add the water, beating until you have a thick cream. Set aside for 2 hours to rest.
2. Make the sauce. Mix the *tahini*, lemon juice, water, tabasco sauce and salt together and

stir until smooth. Pour into a sauce boat for the table.
3. Boil the cauliflower florets in a little salted water for 2-3 minutes. Drain well.
4. Beat the egg white until stiff and fold into the batter.
5. Heat some oil in a frying pan and when hot, dip the cauliflower into the batter, then fry for 4-5 minutes, in batches if necessary, until golden brown. Keep warm and serve with lemon halves and sauce.

GREEN PEA TART

Baking time:	15 minutes for the pastry, plus 20 minutes for the tart
Cooking time:	10 minutes
Preparation time:	10 minutes
Standing time:	10 minutes

IMPERIAL (METRIC)
½ lb (225g) shortcrust pastry

AMERICAN
8 oz shortcrust pastry

Filling:
1 lb (450g) shelled fresh peas
½ pint (300ml) single cream
Pinch of sea salt, pepper, sugar
2 oz (55g) grated parmesan cheese

1 lb shelled fresh peas
1¼ cupsful light cream
Pinch of sea salt, pepper, sugar
½ cupful grated parmesan cheese

1. Preheat the oven to 375°F/190°C (Gas Mark 5).
2. Line a 9-10½-inch (22.5-26cm) tart tin with the pastry and bake blind for 15 minutes. Remove the pastry shell from the oven, but leave the oven on.
3. Boil the peas until tender. Drain and leave to cool. Blend them to a purée with the cream, salt, pepper and sugar.
4. Pour the pea purée into the tart shell, sprinkle the top with parmesan cheese and bake for 15-20 minutes.
5. Remove the tart from the oven and let it settle for 10 minutes or so. Serve warm.

ARTICHOKES À LA POLITA

Preparation time: 10 minutes
Cooking time: 30 minutes
Standing time: 10 minutes

IMPERIAL (METRIC)

½ lb (225g) shallots or small onions, peeled
4 oz (115g) carrots, diced
1 pint (600ml) lightly salted water
½ lb (225g) tiny new potatoes, cut into quarters
2 14-oz (395g) tins artichoke hearts, drained
4 fl oz (120ml) olive oil
1 tablespoonful flour mixed with 4 tablespoonsful water
1 teaspoonful each: sea salt and freshly ground black pepper
Juice of 3 lemons
2 tablespoonsful chopped fresh dillweed
2 tablespoonsful chopped fresh marjoram

AMERICAN

½ lb shallots or small onions, peeled
¾ cupful diced carrots
2½ cupsful lightly salted water
½ lb tiny new potatoes, cut into quarters
2 14-oz cans artichoke hearts, drained
½ cupful olive oil
1 tablespoonful flour mixed with 4 tablespoonsful water
1 teaspoonful each: sea salt and freshly ground black pepper
Juice of 3 lemons
2 tablespoonsful chopped fresh dillweed
2 tablespoonsful chopped fresh marjoram

1. Place the onions and carrots in a saucepan with the measured water which has been brought to the boil. Boil, then simmer for 10 minutes. Add the potatoes and continue cooking for another 10 minutes.

2. Add the rest of the ingredients except the herbs and cook for 10 minutes more. Stir in the herbs. Remove from the heat and allow to settle. Serve warm.

CATALAN SPINACH

Cooking time: 20 minutes

IMPERIAL (METRIC)	AMERICAN
2 lb (900g) leaf spinach	*2 lb leaf spinach*
2 tablespoonsful olive oil	*2 tablespoonsful olive oil*
4 cloves garlic, crushed	*4 cloves garlic, crushed*
2 tablespoonsful pine nuts	*2 tablespoonsful pine nuts*
1 tablespoonful currants	*1 tablespoonful currants*
1 oz (30g) butter	*2 tablespoonsful butter*
Sea salt and freshly ground black pepper	*Sea salt and freshly ground black pepper*
4 slices dry wholemeal bread	*4 slices dry wholewheat bread*

1. Cook spinach slowly in a covered pan without water. After 10 minutes, drain off the juices and chop the spinach coarsely with a wooden spoon.
2. Heat the olive oil in a pan and add half the garlic, the pine nuts and currants and cook until the pine nuts are golden, stirring frequently. Add the spinach, stir well and season. Keep warm.
3. Melt the butter in another pan and add the rest of the garlic. Cut the bread diagonally in half and fry in the butter until crisp and brown.
4. Pour the spinach into a bowl and place the fried bread croutons around the rim. Serve.

PESCHE RIPIENE (Stuffed Peaches)

Preparation time: 10 minutes
Baking time: 30 minutes

IMPERIAL (METRIC)	AMERICAN
5 peaches	*5 peaches*
2 large macaroons	*2 large macaroons*
12 almonds, peeled and chopped	*12 almonds, peeled and chopped*
1 oz (30g) candied lemon peel, chopped	*3 tablespoonsful chopped candied lemon peel*
1½ oz (40g) caster sugar	*3 tablespoonsful superfine sugar*
2½ fl oz (75ml) white wine	*⅓ cupful white wine*

1. Preheat the oven to 350°F/180°C (Gas Mark 4).
2. Skin peaches by popping them into boiling water for a moment (the skins will slip off easily), then slice in half and remove stones.
3. Crumble the macaroons and put into a blender container with the almonds, lemon peel, sugar and one of the peaches. Blend until smooth.
4. Butter a baking dish. Spoon some of the stuffing into each peach half and place in the baking dish. Pour the wine around the base. Sprinkle with a little more sugar and bake for 30 minutes. Remove from the oven and allow to cool a bit, but serve warm.

SPRING MENU 7

Fennel à la Grecque   Pouilly-Fumé

Faiscedda with Broad Bean Purée   Margaux
Barley and Mushroom Casserole
Watercress, Spinach and Avocado Salad

Brie de Melun Bleu
Brillat-Savarin
Cheddar

Mousse Glacées au Rhum   Monbazillac

FENNEL À LA GRECQUE

Preparation time: 5 minutes
Cooking time: 20 minutes

IMPERIAL (METRIC)	AMERICAN
1 bottle (75cl) dry white wine	*1 bottle dry white wine*
4 tablespoonsful olive oil	*4 tablespoonsful olive oil*
2 tablespoonsful tomato purée	*2 tablespoonsful tomato paste*
Zest and juice of 1 lemon	*Zest and juice of 1 lemon*
1 bay leaf	*1 bay leaf*
1 teaspoonful coriander seeds	*1 teaspoonful coriander seeds*
1 teaspoonful thyme	*1 teaspoonful thyme*
Sea salt and freshly ground black pepper	*Sea salt and freshly ground black pepper*
4 large heads fennel, trimmed and halved	*4 large heads fennels, trimmed and halved*
Lettuce leaves to serve	*Lettuce leaves to serve*
Chopped parsley to garnish	*Chopped parsley to garnish*

1. Combine everything except fennel, lettuce and parsley in a large saucepan and mix well. Bring to the boil. Remove from the heat and add the fennel. Simmer for 15 minutes. Leave to cool.
2. Remove the fennel with a slotted spoon and place in a serving dish. Place the stock back over the heat and boil fiercely to reduce the liquid by two-thirds. Pour the reduced stock over the fennel.
3. Serve on lettuce leaves and garnish with chopped parsley.

FAISCEDDA WITH BROAD BEAN PURÉE (Sardinian Bean Cake)

Preparation time: 10 minutes
Cooking time: 25 minutes

IMPERIAL (METRIC)	AMERICAN
3 lb (1.4kg) broad beans, shelled	*3 lb fava beans, shelled*
6 eggs	*6 eggs*
1 teaspoonful sea salt	*1 teaspoonful sea salt*
½ teaspoonful freshly ground black pepper	*½ teaspoonful freshly ground black pepper*
½ teaspoonful raw cane sugar	*½ teaspoonful raw cane sugar*
1 oz (30g) butter	*2 tablespoonsful butter*
2 tablespoonsful olive oil	*2 tablespoonsful olive oil*
½ pint (300ml) single cream	*1¼ cupsful light cream*

1. Boil the beans until tender. Take half of them and place in a blender with the eggs and half of the salt, pepper and sugar.
2. Blend until smooth and pour into a bowl.
3. Heat the butter and olive oil in a pan, pour the mixture in and cook as for Spanish omelette; that is, over a low heat so that the bottom browns slowly.
4. Heat the grill. When the bottom of the *faiscedda* is done, slip the pan under the grill to cook the top. When the top is brown, remove from the pan onto a baking sheet and keep warm while you prepare the purée.
5. Purée the rest of the beans with the cream and the rest of the seasoning. Heat the purée carefully in a double boiler so that the cream does not boil. When it is hot, pour into a small tureen or sauce boat and serve with the *faiscedda*.

BARLEY AND MUSHROOM CASSEROLE

Cooking time: 25 minutes

IMPERIAL (METRIC)	AMERICAN
2 oz (55g) butter	*4 tablespoonsful butter*
2 oz (55g) finely chopped onion	*⅓ cupful minced onion*
½ lb (225g) mushrooms, thinly sliced	*½ lb mushrooms, thinly sliced*
½ lb (225g) pearl barley	*1⅛ cupsfuls pearl barley*
½ teaspoonful dried marjoram	*½ teaspoonful dried marjoram*
¾ pint (450ml) celery stock (see page 49)	*2 cupsful celery stock (see page 49)*
Sea salt and freshly ground black pepper	*Sea salt and freshly ground black pepper*
Handful of chopped parsley	*Handful of chopped parsley*

1. Heat the butter in a heavy casserole. Cook the onion and mushrooms for a few minutes, then stir in the barley and cook until the barley begins to absorb the pan juices. Add the marjoram, celery stock and seasoning, bring to the boil and simmer for 20 minutes.
2. When the barley is tender, remove the casserole from the heat, turn out into a serving dish and sprinkle with the parsley.

WATERCRESS, SPINACH AND AVOCADO SALAD
Preparation time: 10 minutes

IMPERIAL (METRIC)
3 tablespoonsful walnut oil
Sea salt and freshly ground black
  pepper
1 tablespoonful lemon juice
2 ripe avocados
1 lb (450g) very young leaf spinach
2 bunches watercress

AMERICAN
3 tablespoonsful walnut oil
Sea salt and freshly ground black
  pepper
1 tablespoonful lemon juice
2 ripe avocados
1 lb very young leaf spinach
2 bunches watercress

1. Mix the oil, seasoning and lemon juice together. Place in a mixing bowl.
2. Peel and stone the avocados and slice them into the bowl with the dressing.
3. Wash spinach and watercress. Remove the leaves from the stalks, discard the stalks and tear the leaves into small shreds. Place in a large salad bowl. Pour the avocado and dressing over the leaves. Toss well before serving.

MOUSSE GLACÉ AU RHUM (Iced Rum Mousse)
Preparation time: 15 minutes
Freezing time: 8 hours

IMPERIAL (METRIC)
4 large eggs, separated
5 oz (140g) caster sugar
2½ fl oz (75ml) dark rum
½ pint (300ml) double cream
Boudoir biscuits to serve

AMERICAN
4 large eggs, separated
⅔ cupful superfine sugar
⅓ cupful dark rum
1¼ cupsful heavy cream
Ladyfingers to serve

1. Place the egg yolks, sugar and rum into the top of a double boiler. Cook, stirring, until the mixture becomes a thickish cream.
2. Remove the pan from the heat and continue to stir until cool.
3. Whisk the egg whites until stiff. Whip the cream until stiff. Fold the cream into the egg mixture, then fold the egg whites in, one-third at a time. Pour into a mould and freeze for 8 hours.
4. Spoon the mousse into individual dessert glasses and serve with boudoir biscuits.

SPRING MENU 8

Guacamole	**Californian Chardonnay**
Galette de Choufleur	**Chilean Cabernet Sauvignon**
Sweet Potato Casserole	
French Beans	
Green Salad (See page 30)	
Coleslaw	
Roquefort	
Cheddar	
Chèvre	
Glace des Raisins	**Californian Muscat**

GUACAMOLE (Mexican Avocado Purée)

Preparation time: 15 minutes

IMPERIAL (METRIC)	AMERICAN
3 tomatoes	*3 tomatoes*
2 onions	*2 onions*
1 green pepper	*1 green pepper*
1 green chilli	*1 green chili pepper*
1 tablespoonful lemon juice	*1 tablespoonful lemon juice*
3 tablespoonsful olive oil	*3 tablespoonsful olive oil*
Sea salt and freshly ground black pepper	*Sea salt and freshly ground black pepper*
1 tablespoonful chopped coriander leaves	*1 tablespoonful chopped cilantro*
3-4 very ripe avocados	*3-4 very ripe avocados*

1. Peel the tomatoes by popping them into boiling water for a moment.
2. Chop the tomatoes, onions, green pepper and chilli very finely, then add the lemon juice, olive oil, seasoning and coriander.
3. Cut the avocados in half, stone, scoop out the flesh and reserve the shells. Purée the avocado flesh. (It is best to do this in a blender.)
4. Mix the avocado flesh with the rest of the ingredients and pile some of the mixture into each reserved avocado shell.

GALETTE DE CHOUFLEUR

Preparation time:	15 minutes
Cooking time:	15 minutes for tomato sauce, plus 15 minutes
Baking time:	30 minutes

Hot Tomato Sauce:

IMPERIAL (METRIC)	AMERICAN
2 lb (900g) fresh tomatoes	*2 lb fresh tomatoes*
1-3 dried red chillies (depending on tolerance)	*1-3 dried red chilies (depending on tolerance)*
¼ pint (150ml) red wine	*⅔ cupful red wine*
3 cloves garlic, crushed	*3 cloves garlic, crushed*
Sea salt and freshly ground black pepper	*Sea salt and freshly ground black pepper*
Pinch of sugar (optional)	*Pinch of sugar (optional)*

1. Place all ingredients in a saucepan over a low heat. Cover the pan and cook for about 10 minutes, or until the tomatoes are soft and there is a lot of liquid in the pan. Remove from the heat and cool. Discard the chillies.
2. Put the contents of the saucepan through a sieve. Return the sauce to the pan and bring to the boil. Reduce sauce by about one-half.

Note: Because some tomatoes can be sharper than others, this sauce may need a pinch of sugar. But taste carefully. The sauce should have a bite to it, and not taste sweet.

Galette:

IMPERIAL (METRIC)	AMERICAN
1 pint (600ml) hot tomato sauce	*2½ cupful hot tomato sauce*
Handful of fresh basil, finely chopped	*Handful of fresh basil, finely chopped*
4 oz (115g) leaf spinach	*¼ lb leaf spinach*
2 oz (55g) curd cheese	*¼ cupful curd cheese*
4 oz (115g) grated sage derby cheese	*1 cupful grated vermont sage cheese*
6 eggs, separated	*6 eggs, separated*
Sea salt and freshly ground black pepper	*Sea salt and freshly ground black pepper*
1 teaspoonful summer savory	*1 teaspoonful summer savory*
1 large cauliflower	*1 large cauliflower*

1. First make the tomato sauce, but do not reduce it; the egg yolks will thicken it. Add the basil. Set aside.
2. Cook the spinach by placing it into a pan over a low heat and letting it cook in its own moisture for about 8-10 minutes. Let cool, then blend to a purée with the two cheeses.
3. Add the unbeaten egg whites to the spinach mixture along with the seasoning and summer savory. Set aside.

4. Separate the cauliflower into florets and boil in a little salted water for 2-3 minutes. The cauliflower should still be *al dente*. Drain well.
5. Preheat the oven to 400°F/200°C (Gas Mark 6).
6. Butter a shallow earthenware or pyrex dish and cover the base with the spinach mixture. Arrange the cauliflower florets over the spinach. Mix the egg yolks with the tomato sauce and pour over the cauliflower.
7. Cover the dish with foil and bake for 30 minutes, removing the foil for the last 5 minutes. Serve warm.

SWEET POTATO CASSEROLE

Cooking time: 25 minutes
Preparation time: 5 minutes
Baking time: 20 minutes

IMPERIAL (METRIC)	AMERICAN
2½ lb (1.5kg) sweet potatoes	*2½ lb sweet potatoes*
2½ fl oz (75ml) dry sherry	*⅓ cupful dry sherry*
1 tablespoonful brown sugar	*1 tablespoonful brown sugar*
½ teaspoonful sea salt	*½ teaspoonful sea salt*
Freshly ground black pepper to taste	*Freshly ground black pepper to taste*
3 tablespoonsful butter, softened	*3 tablespoonful butter, softened*
Zest and juice of 1 orange	*Zest and juice of 1 orange*

1. Boil the potatoes in plenty of water for 25 minutes, or until tender. Drain and peel.
2. Mash the potatoes until smooth, adding all the remaining ingredients.
3. Preheat the oven to 400°F/200°C (Gas Mark 6).
4. Place the potato mixture in a buttered baking dish and bake for 20 minutes.

COLESLAW

Preparation time: 10 minutes

IMPERIAL (METRIC)
2 tablespoonsful cider vinegar
4 tablespoonsful olive oil
¼ pint (150ml) natural yogurt
Sea salt and freshly ground black
    pepper
1 small cabbage, grated
2 carrots, grated
1 bunch spring onions, finely
    chopped

AMERICAN
2 tablespoonsful cider vinegar
4 tablespoonsful olive oil
⅔ cupful plain yogurt
Sea salt and freshly ground black
    pepper
1 small cabbage, grated
2 carrots, grated
1 bunch scallions, finely chopped

1. Mix vinegar, oil, yogurt and seasoning together in a large bowl.
2. Add the cabbage, carrots and spring onions (scallions) and toss together in the dressing until the vegetables are well covered.

GLACE DES RAISINS (Grape Ice Cream)

Preparation time: 15 minutes
Cooking time: 10 minutes
Freezing time: 8 hours

IMPERIAL (METRIC)
1 lb (450g) black grapes
3 tablespoonsful caster sugar
3 eggs, separated
1 pint (600ml) double cream
1 tablespoonful cassis

AMERICAN
1 lb black grapes
3 tablespoonsful superfine sugar
3 eggs, separated
2½ cupsful heavy cream
1 tablespoonful cassis

1. Place the grapes in a blender container and purée, then press through a sieve, discarding the skins and pips.
2. Heat the grape juice with the sugar and reduce by one-third. When cool, stir in the egg yolks.
3. Whisk the egg whites until stiff. Whip the cream until stiff.
4. Add the cassis to the grape mixture, then fold in the cream and egg whites. Freeze for 8 hours.

SPRING MENU 9

Crudités with Hummous and Jajiki	Rosé d'Anjou
Avocado Flan	Savennières
Marinated Haricot Beans	
Green Salad with Courgettes	
New Potatoes with Mint (See page 61)	
Taleggio	
Dolcelatte	
Pecorino	
Banana and Date Cream	Arak

CRUDITÉS

Preparation time: 20 minutes

Choose a selection of Spring vegetables, sliced finely and arranged on a platter; eg, green and red peppers, mushrooms, spring onions, cauliflower, baby carrots, strips of fennel, cucumbers, tomatoes. Make sure vegetables are very fresh and in prime conditon. The vegetables can be dipped into the two purées.

Hummous (Chickpea Purée):

Soaking time: overnight
Cooking time: 2 hours
Preparation time: 5 minutes

IMPERIAL (METRIC)	AMERICAN
6 oz (170g) chickpeas	*¾ cupful chick peas (garbanzo beans)*
Juice of 1 lemon	*Juice of 1 lemon,*
3 cloves garlic, crushed	*3 cloves garlic, crushed*
Handful of chopped mint	*Handful of chopped mint*
Sea salt and freshly ground black pepper	*Sea salt and freshly ground black pepper*
¼ pint (150ml) olive oil	*⅔ cupful olive oil*

1. Soak chickpeas overnight. Drain, then cook in plenty of boiling salted water for up to 2 hours (20 minutes in a pressure cooker). They are done when the point of a knife causes them to fall apart. Drain, but reserve about ¾ pint/450ml/2 cupful cooking liquor.
2. Put chickpeas in a blender container with the reserved liquor, lemon juice, garlic, mint and seasoning. Blend. Add the olive oil and blend again for up to 2 minutes to get a smooth texture. Place the mixture in a bowl to serve.

Jajiki (Cucumber and Yogurt Sauce):
Preparation time: 5 minutes
Standing time: 1-2 hours

IMPERIAL (METRIC)	AMERICAN
1 large cucumber, peeled and deseeded	*1 large cucumber, peeled and seeded*
¼ pint (150ml) natural yogurt	*⅔ cupful plain yogurt*
Sea salt and freshly ground black pepper	*Sea salt and freshly ground black pepper*
Handful of chopped mint	*Handful of chopped mint*

1. Dice the cucumber into small pieces, place in a colander and sprinkle with salt. Leave for 1-2 hours. Rinse well under cold water and squeeze dry.
2. Mix the yogurt with the salt, pepper and mint. Stir in the cucumber. Place in a bowl to serve.

AVOCADO FLAN

Preparation time: Making the pastry case, plus 20 minutes
Standing time: 1 hour or more

IMPERIAL (METRIC)	AMERICAN
2 egg yolks	*2 egg yolks*
½ pint (300ml) sunflower oil	*1¼ cupsful sunflower oil*
2 cloves garlic, crushed	*2 cloves garlic, crushed*
3 avocados, peeled and stoned	*3 avocados, peeled and stoned*
3 oz (85g) curd cheese	*6 tablespoonsful curd cheese*
3 oz (85g) cottage cheese	*6 tablespoonsful cottage cheese*
1 baked wholemeal pastry case	*1 baked wholewheat pastry case*
Sea salt and freshly ground black pepper	*Sea salt and freshly ground black pepper*
12 stoned black olives, halved	*12 pitted black olives, halved*
Watercress to garnish	*Watercress to garnish*

1. Make a mayonnaise with the egg yolks, oil and garlic. Purée half of one avocado and beat the purée into the mayonnaise.
2. Combine the curd and cottage cheese and add about one-third of the mayonnaise. Spoon this mixture into the base of the pastry case.
3. Slice the rest of the avocados and arrange them over the cheese mixture. (There should be enough to fill the case.) Season with salt and pepper. Spoon the rest of the mayonnaise on top of the avocados, decorate with the olives and garnish with watercress. Let the flan rest for an hour or more before serving.

MARINATED HARICOT BEANS

Soaking time: overnight
Cooking time: 1½-2 hours
Marinating time: 24 hours

IMPERIAL (METRIC)
½ lb (225g) dried haricot beans
1½ pints (900ml) water
2 cloves garlic
6 tablespoonsful olive oil
2 bay leaves

Marinade:
6 tablespoonsful olive oil
6 tablespoonsful wine vinegar
½ teaspoonful each: dried oregano,
   basil, marjoram, tarragon
5 tablespoonsful chopped parsley
Sea salt and freshly ground black
   pepper

AMERICAN
1 cupful dried navy beans
3¾ cupsful water
2 cloves garlic
6 tablespoonsful olive oil
2 bay leaves

6 tablespoonsful olive oil
6 tablespoonsful wine vinegar
½ teaspoonful each: dried oregano,
   basil, marjoram, tarragon
⅓ cupful chopped parsley
Sea salt and freshly ground black
   pepper

1. Soan beans overnight. Drain, then boil in the measured water with the garlic, oil and bay leaves for 1½-2 hours or until tender. Drain.
2. Mix all the marinade ingredients together. Pour into the still-warm beans, cover the bowl and leave for 24 hours.

GREEN SALAD WITH COURGETTES

Preparation time: 5 minutes

IMPERIAL (METRIC)
3 courgettes
3 tablespoonsful olive oil
1 teaspoonful umbeshi vinegar (see
   note)
1 teaspoonful raspberry vinegar
Sea salt and freshly ground black
   pepper
3 crisp lettuce hearts

AMERICAN
3 zucchini
3 tablespoonsful olive oil
1 teaspoonful umbeshi vinegar (see
   note)
1 teaspoonful raspberry vinegar
Sea salt and freshly ground black
   pepper
3 crisp lettuce hearts

1. Slice the courgettes (zucchini) thinly. Blanch them in boiling water for about 1 minute. Drain.
2. Mix oil, vinegars and seasoning together in a large salad bowl. Cut the lettuce into quarters and add to the bowl. Pile the courgettes in the centre. Toss well before serving.

Note: Japanese umbeshi vinegar, made from fermented plums, can be purchased at Oriental shops and some delicatessens.

BANANA AND DATE CREAM

Preparation time: 10 minutes
Chilling time: Up to 5 hours

IMPERIAL (METRIC)
5 bananas
½ lb (225g) fresh or dried dates,
   stoned
½ pint (300ml) single cream

AMERICAN
5 bananas
½ lb fresh or dried dates, pitted
1¼ cupsful light cream

1.   Peel and thinly slice the bananas. Cut dates in half. Arrange alternate layers of bananas and dates in a bowl. Pour the cream over the fruit and refrigerate for up to 5 hours.

SPRING MENU 10

Potage aux Cerises   Beaujolais-Villages

Tourte de Légumes Verts   Gewürtztraminer
Risi e Bisi
Purée de Choufleur
Mixed Green Salad

Chabichou Fermier
Stilton

Glace au Chocolat   Monbazillac

POTAGE AUX CERISES (Cherry Soup)

Preparation time: 15 minutes
Cooking time: 35 minutes

IMPERIAL (METRIC)	AMERICAN
2 lb (900g) ripe black cherries	*2 lb ripe black cherries*
2 oz (55g) butter	*4 tablespoonsful butter*
1 teaspoonful ground coriander	*1 teaspoonful ground coriander*
2 teaspoonsful flour	*2 teaspoonsful flour*
1 bottle (75cl) red wine	*1 bottle red wine*
Sea salt and freshly ground black pepper	*Sea salt and freshly ground black pepper*
6-8 slices French bread, fried in garlic and butter	*6-8 slices French bread, fried in garlic and butter*

1. Remove stems from cherries and stone.
2. Melt the butter in a saucepan. Add the coriander and cherries. Cook over a low heat until cherries have softened.
3. Sprinkle with flour and stir well. Cook for another moment or two. Add the wine, salt and pepper. Bring to the boil and simmer for 30 minutes.
4. Prepare the French bread croûtons. Place a croûton on the bottom of each soup bowl and pour the soup over.

TOURTE DE LÉGUMES VERTS (Green Vegetable Mould)

Preparation time: 15 minutes
Cooking time: 20 minutes
Baking time: 45-55 minutes

IMPERIAL (METRIC)
1 cabbage
1 lb (450g) leeks
3 oz (85g) butter
1 lb (450g) French beans
½ lb (225g) mushrooms, sliced
Sea salt and freshly ground black
  pepper

AMERICAN
1 cabbage
1 lb leeks
6 tablespoonsful butter
1 lb green beans
½ lb mushrooms, sliced
Sea salt and freshly ground black
  pepper

Custard:
2 eggs, plus 2 egg yolks
¼ pint (150ml) milk
¾ pint (450ml) double cream
Sea salt and freshly ground black
  pepper
Pinch of grated nutmeg

2 eggs, plus 2 egg yolks
⅔ cupful milk
2 cupsful heavy cream
Sea salt and freshly ground black
  pepper
Pinch of grated nutmeg

1. Remove the cabbage leaves from the core and discard the core and the central ribs from the leaves. Boil the cabbage leaves in plenty of salted water for about 5 minutes, or until tender. Drain well in a colander.
2. Clean leeks, cut them in half lengthways, then into 1-inch (2.5cm) chunks. Cook them in 4 tablespoonsful butter in a covered saucepan so that they steam in their own liquid for about 4 minutes. Cool.
3. Cook the beans in boiling water for 5-7 minutes. Drain well.
4. Cook the mushrooms in 2 tablespoonsful butter until soft.
5. Make the custard. Beat the eggs and egg yolks with the milk and cream until smooth. Season well with salt, pepper and nutmeg.
6. Preheat the oven to 350°F/180°C (Gas Mark 4).
7. Butter a 9-inch (22.5cm) cake tin, *moule à manque* or soufflé dish and line the bottom and sides of the mould with the cabbage leaves, leaving enough hanging over the top to cover the filling. Chop the remaining cabbage leaves.
8. Place a layer of mushrooms on the bottom of the mould, then a layer of leeks, then beans and finally cabbage, seasoning each layer with salt and pepper. Continue until the mould is full.
7. Pour in enough custard to come up to the top of the vegetables. Fold over the cabbage leaves and bake for 45-55 minutes, or until the custard is set. Allow to stand for 5 minutes before turning out onto a serving dish.

RISI E BISI (Spring Pea Risotto)

Preparation time: 5 minutes
Cooking time: 20 minutes

IMPERIAL (METRIC)
1 onion
3 oz (85g) butter
½ lb (225g) patna rice
1½ pints (900ml) vegetable stock
1 lb (450g) peas, shelled
Sea salt and freshly ground black
   pepper
2 oz (55g) freshly grated parmesan
   cheese

AMERICAN
1 onion
6 tablespoonsful butter
1 cupful patna rice
3¾ cupsful vegetable stock
1 lb peas, shelled
Sea salt and freshly ground black
   pepper
½ cupful freshly grated parmesan
   cheese

1. Chop the onion finely and cook in two-thirds of the butter until soft.
2. Add the rice. Stir well. Cook for a moment until the rice has absorbed some of the butter, then add half the stock. Bring to the boil, cover the pan, reduce the heat to very low and cook for about 20 minutes.
3. In the meantime, cook the peas in the remaining stock for about 15 minutes.
4. When the rice is cooked, add the peas. Season with salt and pepper, pour into a serving dish, add the remaining butter and sprinkle with parmesan cheese.

PURÉE DE CHOUFLEUR

Preparation time: 10 minutes
Cooking time: 10 minutes

IMPERIAL (METRIC)
1 large cauliflower
Sea salt and freshly ground black
   pepper
Pinch of grated nutmeg
2 tablespoonsful double cream
1 oz (30g) butter

AMERICAN
1 large cauliflower
Sea salt and freshly ground black
   pepper
Pinch of grated nutmeg
2 tablespoonsful heavy cream
2 tablespoonsful butter

1. Separate cauliflower into florets. Discard the central core and boil the cauliflower in salted water for about 7 minutes. Drain well.
2. Blend cauliflower to a purée and add seasoning, nutmeg and cream. Reheat gently, then pour into an earthenware dish, dot with the butter and keep warm in the oven.

MIXED GREEN SALAD
Preparation time: 10 minutes

IMPERIAL (METRIC)	AMERICAN
1 lettuce	*1 lettuce*
1 head curly endive	*1 head chicory*
2 heads chicory	*2 heads Belgian endive*
1 green pepper	*1 green pepper*
Sea salt and freshly ground black pepper	*Sea salt and freshly ground black pepper*
2 tablespoonsful olive oil	*2 tablespoonsful olive oil*
1 tablespoonful wine vinegar	*1 tablespoonful wine vinegar*

1. Wash all the vegetables and drain.
2. Make the dressing and place in the bottom of a salad bowl.
3. Mix lettuce leaves and curly endive (chicory) together and add to the bowl.
4. Separate the chicory (endive) leaves and place upright around the sides of the bowl.
5. Deseed pepper and slice into thin rings. Scatter over the lettuce and endive (chicory). The salad may be tossed at the table before serving.

GLACE AU CHOCOLAT (Chocolate Ice Cream)
Cooking time: 15 minutes
Cooling time: 30 minutes
Freezing time: 2-4 hours

IMPERIAL (METRIC)	AMERICAN
7 oz (200g) dark bitter chocolate, grated or chopped into small bits	*1½ cupsful grated or chopped dark bitter chocolate*
¾ pint (450ml) milk	*2 cupsful milk*
5 egg yolks	*5 egg yolks*
4 oz (115g) caster sugar	*½ cupful superfine sugar*
¾ pint (450ml) double cream	*2 cupsful heavy cream*

1. Melt the chocolate in a bowl over hot water. Bring milk almost to the boil.
2. Beat the egg yolks with the sugar until thick and light.
3. Whisk half of the hot milk into the egg yolks, then whisk the mixture back into the remaining milk.
4. Heat gently, stirring with a wooden spoon until the custard thickens slightly. Remove from the heat and stir in the chocolate. Allow to cool.
5. Whip the cream lightly, beat into the custard and freeze for 2-4 hours.

SPRING MENU 11

Poireaux Vinaigrette	Crépy
Charlotte d'Aubergines	Coufran
Stuffed Cucumbers	
Salade Italienne	
Green Salad (See page 30)	
Saint-Nectaire	
Saint-Remy	
	Muscat de
Soufflé Chaud au Citron	Frontignan

POIREAUX VINAIGRETTE (Leeks Vinaigrette)

Preparation time: 10 minutes
Cooking time: 15 minutes

IMPERIAL (METRIC)	AMERICAN
12-16 small leeks	*12-16 small leeks*
2 tablespoonsful white wine vinegar	*2 tablespoonsful white wine vinegar*
6 tablespoonsful olive oil	*6 tablespoonsful olive oil*
1 egg yolk	*1 egg yolk*
2 shallots, finely diced	*2 shallots, finely diced*
2 tablespoonsful chopped parsley	*2 tablespoonsful chopped parsley*
2 hard-boiled eggs, finely chopped	*2 hard-cooked eggs, finely chopped*
Sea salt and freshly ground black	*Sea salt and freshly ground black*
* pepper*	* pepper*

1. Cut leeks in half lengthways and trim away the green leaves. Wash under a running tap, then steam leeks until tender, about 15 minutes.
2. Mix the vinegar, oil and egg yolk together. Add the shallots, parsley, hard-boiled eggs and seasoning. Beat well.
3. Arrange the leeks on individual plates, alternating tops and bottoms, allowing 4 halves per person. Pour the vinaigrette over.

CHARLOTTE D'AUBERGINES

Preparation time: 15 minutes
Standing time: 1 hour
Cooking time: 30 minutes
Baking time: 50 minutes

IMPERIAL (METRIC)	AMERICAN
1¾ lb (790g) aubergines	*2 large eggplants*
2 lb (900g) tomatoes	*2 lb tomatoes*
¼ pint (150ml) olive oil	*⅔ cupful olive oil*
1 large onion, finely chopped	*1 large onion, minced*
3 cloves garlic, crushed	*3 cloves garlic, crushed*
Sea salt and freshly ground black pepper	*Sea salt and freshly ground black pepper*
½ pint (300ml) natural yogurt	*1¼ cupsful plain yogurt*
½ pint (300ml) vegetable stock	*1¼ cupsful vegetable stock*

1. Trim aubergines (eggplants) and cut into ¾-inch (2cm) slices. Sprinkle with salt and leave for 1 hour, to get rid of the bitter juices. Rinse well under cold water, drain and pat dry.
2. Peel and chop the tomatoes. Heat 2 tablespoonsful of the olive oil in a pan and sauté the onion and garlic until soft. Add the tomatoes and simmer for about 20 minutes, until the mixture is thick.
3. Heat the rest of the oil in another pan and brown the aubergines on both sides. Season with salt and pepper.
4. Preheat the oven to 350°F/180°C (Gas Mark 4).
5. Butter an 8-inch (20cm) cake tin, soufflé dish or 2-pint/1-litre/5-cup charlotte mould. Arrange a layer of overlapping aubergine slices on the bottom and up the sides of the mould. Take about one-third of the tomato mixture and set aside. Spread the aubergines with a little of the remaining tomato mixture, then some yogurt. Continue layering the aubergine, tomato and yogurt, ending with a layer of aubergine.
6. Mix the reserved tomato mixture with the vegetable stock to make a sauce.
7. Cover the mould with foil and bake for 50 minutes. Cool a little, then unmould onto a serving plate. Heat the sauce and spoon it over the charlotte.

STUFFED CUCUMBERS

Preparation time: 15 minutes
Cooking time: 15 minutes
Baking time: 30 minutes

IMPERIAL (METRIC)	AMERICAN
2 large cucumbers	*2 large cucumbers*

Stuffing:

½ lb (225g) shallots or spring onions	*½ lb shallots or scallions*
1 oz (30g) butter	*2 tablespoonsful butter*
Handful of chopped parsley	*Handful of chopped parsley*
Sea salt and freshly ground black pepper	*Sea salt and freshly ground black pepper*
1 egg, beaten	*1 egg, beaten*
3 tablespoonsful breadcrumbs	*3 tablespoonsful bread crumbs*

Mornay Sauce:

1 oz (30g) butter	*2 tablespoonsful butter*
1 oz (30g) flour	*¼ cupful flour*
Sea salt and freshly ground black pepper	*Sea salt and freshly ground black pepper*
½ pint (300ml) milk	*1¼ cupsful milk*
3 oz (85g) double gloucester cheese, grated	*¾ cupful grated double gloucester or* cheddar *cheese*
1 oz (30g) grated gruyère cheese	*¼ cupful grated unprocessed gruyère cheese*

1. Peel the cucumbers in strips so they are pleasantly striped. Cut into 4-inch (10cm) pieces, then in half, lengthways. Scoop out all the seeds and discard. Boil the cucumbers for only 4 minutes. Drain well.
2. Slice the shallots or spring onions (scallions) and sauté in the butter until soft. Remove from the heat. When cool, add the parsley, seasoning, egg and enough breadcrumbs to hold the mixture together.
3. Preheat the oven to 350°F/180°C (Gas Mark 4).
4. Place the cucumbers in a buttered baking dish and spoon the stuffing into the shells. Bake for 10-15 minutes or until the stuffing has set. The stuffed cucumbers can now be left for up to 24 hours and finished after the sauce is made. If you are going to make the sauce immediately, leave the oven on.
5. Make the sauce. Melt the butter, add the flour and let the roux cook over a low heat for a minute or two. Season and add the milk slowly, then add the cheese and stir until the sauce is smooth.
6. Mask the stuffed cucumbers with the sauce and bake for about 15 minutes, until the sauce is browned.

SALADE ITALIENNE

Preparation time: 5 minutes
Cooking time: 15 minutes

IMPERIAL (METRIC)	AMERICAN
6 oz (170g) dried pasta shells	*2 cupsful dried pasta shells*
4 oz (115g) mushrooms, sliced	*1½ cupsful sliced mushrooms*
1 oz (30g) green peppercorns	*2 tablespoonsful green peppercorns*
2 oz (55g) butter	*4 tablespoonsful butter*
4 oz (55g) stoned black olives, halved	*1 cupful pitted black olives, halved*
Sea salt and freshly ground black pepper	*Sea salt and freshly ground black pepper*

1. Cook the pasta in plenty of boiling salted water until tender, about 15 minutes.
2. Meanwhile, sauté the mushrooms and green peppercorns in the butter. When soft, add the olives. Stir well. Increase the heat and let the liquid evaporate.
3. Drain the pasta well. Mix with the other ingredients, season to taste and pour into a serving dish.

SOUFFLÉ CHAUD AU CITRON (Hot Lemon Soufflé)

Cooking time: 15 minutes
Preparation time: 15 minutes
Baking time: 10 minutes

IMPERIAL (METRIC)	AMERICAN
2½ oz (40g) butter	*5 tablespoonsful butter*
4 oz (115g) caster sugar	*½ cupful superfine sugar*
6 tablespoonsful lemon juice	*6 tablespoonsful lemon juice*
4 egg yolks	*4 egg yolks*
Zest of 2 lemons	*Zest of 2 lemons*
5 egg whites	*5 egg whites*
Icing sugar	*Confectioner's sugar*

1. Butter a 1½-pint/1-litre/1-quart soufflé dish with 1 tablespoonful butter, sprinkle with sugar and discard any excess. Preheat the oven to 425°F/220°C (Gas Mark 7).
2. Heat the remaining butter in a pan with half the sugar and all the lemon juice until butter is melted and sugar is dissolved. Remove from the heat and beat in the egg yolks, one at a time. Add the lemon zest. Heat gently, whisking all the time, until the mixture thickens to the consistency of double cream. Remove from the heat.
3. Whisk the egg whites until stiff. Add the remaining sugar and continue beating until glossy.
4. Gently reheat the lemon mixture until it is hot, then fold in some of the egg whites. Add this mixture to the remaining egg whites and fold together as lightly as possible.
5. Spoon the mixture into the prepared soufflé dish and bake at once for 9-10 minutes or until the soufflé is puffy and brown. Sprinkle with icing sugar and serve immediately.

SPRING MENU 12

Fasoulia	**Red Rioja Reserva**
Gâteau d'Épinards	**Meursault**
Pommes de Terre en Matelote	
Salade de Courgettes	
Mixed Green Salad (See page 94)	
Bleu de Sassenage	
Cheddar	
Cherry Fool	**Sweet Champagne**

FASOULIA (Greek Bean Salad)

Soaking time: overnight
Cooking time: 2 ½ hours
Cooling time: 1 hour

IMPERIAL (METRIC)	AMERICAN
¾ lb (340g) dried haricot beans	*1½ cupsful dried navy beans*
¼ pint (150ml) olive oil	*⅔ cupful olive oil*
5 cloves garlic, crushed	*5 cloves garlic, crushed*
1 bay leaf	*1 bay leaf*
Pinch of thyme and sage	*Pinch of thyme and sage*
1 teaspoonful oregano	*1 teaspoonful oregano*
2 tablespoonsful tomato purée	*2 tablespoonsful tomato paste*
1 onion, thinly sliced	*1 onion, thinly sliced*
Juice of 1 lemon	*Juice of 1 lemon*
Sea salt and freshly ground black pepper	*Sea salt and freshly ground black pepper*

1. Soak the beans overnight. Drain and discard the water.
2. Boil the beans over a high heat for 10 minutes. Drain.
3. Heat the olive oil in a thick-bottomed saucepan. Add the beans, garlic, bay leaf, thyme, sage and oregano. Simmer for up to 10 minutes to allow the beans to soak up the oil and herbs, then add enough boiling water to cover the beans by 2 inches (5cm). Stir in the tomato purée, cover the pan and cook the beans very slowly for about 2 hours. Watch carefully and add more water if they are drying out.
4. When the beans are tender, add the onion and lemon juice. Stir into the beans, cover the saucepan and remove from the heat. Leave for about 10 minutes for the onion to soften a little in the warmth of the pan. Season to taste.
5. Serve cold, not chilled. This dish can be prepared 1 or 2 days in advance.

GÂTEAU D'ÉPINARDS (Spinach Gâteau)

Preparation time: 15 minutes
Cooking time: 45 minutes
Baking time: 10 minutes

IMPERIAL (METRIC)	AMERICAN
2 lb (900g) leaf spinach	*2 lb leaf spinach*
2 tablespoonsful double cream	*2 tablespoonsful heavy cream*
1 oz (30g) butter	*2 tablespoonsful butter*

Sauce:

1 tablespoonful oil	*1 tablespoonful oil*
1 oz (30g) butter	*2 tablespoonsful butter*
1 carrot, finely chopped	*1 carrot, finely chopped*
1 onion, finely chopped	*1 onion, minced*
1 stalk celery, finely chopped	*1 stalk celery, finly chopped*
1 14-oz (390g) tin tomatoes	*1 14-oz can tomatoes*
4 oz (115g) fresh peas, cooked	*¾ cupful fresh peas, cooked*
Sea salt and freshly ground black pepper	*Sea salt and freshly ground black pepper*

Omelettes:

6 eggs, beaten	*6 eggs, beaten*
4 oz (115g) grated gruyère cheese	*1 cupful grated unprocessed gruyère cheese*
4 tablespoonsful double cream	*4 tablespoonsful heavy cream*
Sea salt and freshly ground black pepper	*Sea salt and freshly ground black pepper*
Pinch of nutmeg	*Pinch of nutmeg*

1. Cook the spinach without water in a large pan over a low heat. In about 10 minutes, it will have reduced in bulk by two-thirds and be tender. Remove from the heat and chop finely with a wooden spoon. Discard any fibrous stalks. Drain, add cream and butter and cook for a further 10 minutes until you have a thick purée. Set aside.
2. Heat the oil and butter in a frying pan and sauté the carrot, onion and celery until soft. Add the tomatoes and peas and continue to simmer for about 15 minutes. Remove from the heat and season to taste.
3. Make the omelettes. Add the cheese, cream, seasoning and nutmeg to the beaten eggs. Divide the mixture into thirds and make 3 separate omelettes.
4. Preheat the oven to 400°F/200°C (Gas Mark 6).
5. Assemble the gateau. Place one omelette in a round cake tin or soufflé dish. Cover with some sauce, then spinach. Do the same for the other omelettes, ending with the spinach on top.
6. Bake for 10 minutes.

POMMES DE TERRE EN MATELOTE (Potatoes with Parsley and Chive Sauce)

Preparation time: 5 minutes
Cooking time: 15 minutes

IMPERIAL (METRIC)	AMERICAN
2 lb (900g) peeled, boiled potatoes	*2 lb peeled, boiled potatoes*
2 oz (55g) butter	*4 tablespoonsful butter*
½ pint (300ml) vegetable stock	*1¼ cupsful vegetable stock*
½ pint (300ml) white wine	*1¼ cupsful white wine*
Sea salt and freshly ground black	*Sea salt and freshly ground black*
* pepper*	* pepper*
Handful of chopped parsley	*Handful of chopped parsley*
Handful of chopped chives	*Handful of chopped chives*
2 egg yolks	*2 egg yolks*

1. Cut the potatoes into quarters. Melt the butter in a large pan and add the stock and wine. Add the potatoes, salt, pepper and herbs. Bring to the boil and simmer for 10 minutes.
2. Mix the egg yolks together in a bowl. Drain off the sauce and beat into the egg yolks, then return the sauce to the pan and cook for a further few minutes until the sauce thickens.

SALADE DE COURGETTES

Preparation time: 5 minutes
Cooking time: 7 minutes

IMPERIAL (METRIC)	AMERICAN
1 lb (450g) small courgettes	*1 lb small zucchini*
4 tablespoonsful olive oil	*4 tablespoonsful olive oil*
2 shallots, finely chopped	*2 shallots, minced*
1½ teaspoonsful paprika	*1½ teaspoonsful paprika*
Sea salt and freshly ground black	*Sea salt and freshly ground black*
* pepper*	* pepper*
1½ teaspoonsful raw cane sugar	*½ teaspoonful raw cane sugar*
1 teaspoonful dillweed	*1 teaspoonful dillweed*
3 tablespoonsful white wine vinegar	*3 tablespoonsful white wine vinegar*

1. Trim the courgettes (zucchini) and slice them thinly.
2. Heat the oil. Add the shallots and courgettes and cook over a low heat, stirring from time to time, about 5 minutes. They must not brown, just soften a little.
3. Add the rest of the ingredients and cook for a further 2 minutes.
4. Transfer to a serving dish. This salad can be eaten hot, warm or cool.

CHERRY FOOL

Preparation time: 10 minutes
Cooking time: 10 minutes
Chilling time: 2 hours

IMPERIAL (METRIC)
2 lb (900g) ripe, black cherries
3 tablespoonsful caster sugar
¼ pint (150ml) red wine
½ pint (300ml) double cream

AMERICAN
2 lb ripe, black cherries
3 tablespoonsful superfine sugar
⅔ cupful red wine
1¼ cupsful heavy cream

1. Stone the cherries. Place them in a pan with the sugar and wine. Bring to the boil and simmer for about 10 minutes. Cool, then blend to a purée. Sieve.
2. Whip the cream until stiff. Combine cream and cherry purée and pile into individual glasses. Refrigerate for 2 hours or more.

SPRING MENU 13

Oeufs en Matelote	Beaujolais-Villages
Stilton Quiche	Châteauneuf-du-Pape
Hot Spiced Beetroot	
Pommes de Terre à la Manière D'Apt	
Mixed Green Salad (See page 94)	
Belval	
Boulette de Cambrai	
Melon with Muscat de Beaumes-de-Venise	

OEUFS EN MATELOTE (Wine-Poached Eggs)

Preparation time: 5 minutes
Cooking time: 10 minutes

IMPERIAL (METRIC)	AMERICAN
6-8 slices French bread	*6-8 slices French bread*
Butter for frying	*Butter for frying*
2 cloves garlic, crushed	*2 cloves garlic, crushed*
½ pint (300ml) red wine	*1¼ cupsful red wine*
2 cloves garlic, sliced	*2 cloves garlic, sliced*
Pinch of sea salt	*Pinch of sea salt*
Bouquet garni	*Bouquet garni*
6-8 eggs	*6-8 eggs*

1. Fry the slices of French bread in butter and crushed garlic until they are crisp and golden. Keep warm in the oven.
2. Heat the wine with the sliced garlic, salt and bouquet garni. Boil for 3 minutes, then remove the garlic and bouquet garni.
3. Poach the eggs in the wine until the whites are just set. Place each one on a slice of fried bread and serve.

STILTON QUICHE

Preparation time: Making pastry case, plus 10 minutes
Baking time: 30 minutes

IMPERIAL (METRIC)
3 oz (85g) Stilton cheese
3 oz (85g) cream cheese
3 oz (85g) curd cheese
2 oz (55g) butter
3 eggs
¾ pint (450ml) single cream
Sea salt, freshly ground black
 pepper
Pinch of cayenne pepper
1 tablespoonful chopped spring
 onions
1 tablespoonful chopped parsley
1 baked pastry case (see page 22)

AMERICAN
3 oz Stilton or other blue-veined
 cheese
1 3-oz package cream cheese
4 tablespoonsful curd cheese
4 tablespoonsful butter
3 eggs
2 cupsful light cream
Sea salt, freshly ground black
 pepper
Pinch of cayenne pepper
1 tablespoonful chopped scallions
1 tablespoonful chopped parsley
1 baked pastry case (see page 22)

1. Preheat the oven to 400°F/200°C (Gas Mark 6).
2. Put all the cheese, butter, eggs and cream in a blender container and blend until smooth. Add salt, pepper, cayenne pepper, spring onions and parsley and blend for another moment to mix well. Pour into the baked pastry case.
3. Bake for 30 minutes.

HOT SPICED BEETROOT

Preparation time: 5 minutes
Cooking time: 5 minutes

IMPERIAL (METRIC)
1½ lb (680g) cooked beetroot
4 tablespoonsful soured cream
2 tablespoonsful wine vinegar
½ teaspoonful tabasco sauce
1 tablespoonful capers
1 tablespoonful green peppercorns
Sea salt and freshly ground black
 pepper

AMERICAN
1½ lb cooked beets
4 tablespoonsful sour cream
2 tablespoonsful wine vinegar
½ teaspoonful tabasco sauce
1 tablespoonful capers
1 tablespoonful green peppercorns
Sea salt and freshly ground black
 pepper

1. Peel beetroot and cut into small dice. Place into a saucepan with the rest of the ingredients. Heat gently and serve.

POMMES DE TERRE À LA MANIÈRE D'APT (Potato Gratin)

Preparation time: 10 minutes
Cooking time: 35 minutes
Baking time: 30 minutes

IMPERIAL (METRIC)
2 lb (900g) potatoes
4 tablespoonsful olive oil
5 tablespoonsful tomato purée
Sea salt and freshly ground black
   pepper
1 bay leaf
12 stoned black olives
3 tablespoonsful wholemeal
   breadcrumbs

AMERICAN
2 lb potatoes
4 tablespoonsful olive oil
1 small can tomato paste
Sea salt and freshly ground black
   pepper
1 bay leaf
12 pitted black olives
3 tablespoonsful wholewheat bread
   crumbs

1. Peel potatoes and cut into ¼-inch (0.5cm) slices.
2. Heat olive oil in a casserole. Add the tomato purée, salt, pepper, bay leaf and potatoes and simmer for 5 minutes.
3. Add enough boiling water to cover potatoes and simmer for another 30 minutes. Meanwhile, preheat the oven to 350°F/180°C (Gas Mark 4).
4. Add the black olives to the casserole and cover with a layer of breadcrumbs. Bake for 30 minutes.

MELON WITH MUSCAT DE BEAUMES-DE-VENISE

Preparation time: 10 minutes
Standing time: 30 minutes

IMPERIAL (METRIC)
3-4 Ogen or Charentais melons, chilled
1 bottle (75cl) Muscat de Beaumes-de-Venise

AMERICAN
3-4 cantaloupes or casaba melons, chilled
1 bottle Muscat de Beaumes-de-Venise

1. Slice melons in half and deseed. Place each half on a plate and fill the cavity with the wine. Leave to rest for 30 minutes, then serve.

SUMMER MENUS

SUMMER MENU 1

Avocado Mousse	**Sauvignon Blanc**
Roulade d'Épinards **Courgettes, Carrots and Tomatoes** **New Potatoes with Mint** **Mixed Green Salad (See page 94)**	**Côtes-du-Rhône**
Chabichou Fermier **Emmental** **Brie de Meaux**	
Melon Salad	**Muscat**

AVOCADO MOUSSE

Preparation time: 15 minutes
Chilling time: 2 hours

IMPERIAL (METRIC)
3 ripe avocados
2 oz (55g) butter, melted
½ pint (300ml) double cream
½ teaspoonful sea salt and white
  pepper
4 egg whites (reserve yolks for next
  recipe)
2 tablespoonsful capers
Parsley to garnish

AMERICAN
3 ripe avocados
4 tablespoonsful melted butter
1¼ cupsful heavy cream
½ teaspoonful sea salt and white
  pepper
4 egg whites (reserve yolks for next
  recipe)
2 tablespoonsful capers
Parsley to garnish

1. Cut avocados in half and remove stones. Scoop out all the flesh and place in a blender container. Add the melted butter, cream, salt and pepper. Blend until smooth.
2. Whisk the egg whites until stiff. Fold into the avocado purée and add the capers. Mix well. Place in a serving dish and refrigerate for 2 hours. Garnish with chopped parsley and parsley sprigs before serving.

ROULADE D'ÉPINARDS (Spinach Roulade)

Preparation time: 20 minutes
Cooking time: 10 minutes
Baking time: 20 minutes

IMPERIAL (METRIC)	AMERICAN
Roulade:	
14 oz (395g) leaf spinach	*1 lb leaf spinach*
7 oz (200g) fresh sorrel	*¼ lb fresh sorrel*
1 tablespoonful flour	*1 tablespoonful flour*
4 eggs, separated, plus 4 egg yolks	*4 eggs, separated, plus 4 egg yolks*
4 oz (115g) double gloucester or sage derby cheese, grated	*1 cupful grated cheddar or vermont sage cheese*
Filling:	
¼ pint (150ml) milk, infused with bay leaves, shallots and 5 peppercorns	*⅔ cupful milk, infused with bay leaves, shallots and 5 peppercorns*
1 tablespoonful flour	*1 tablespoonful flour*
1½ oz (40g) butter, softened	*3 tablespoonsful butter, softened*
3 tablespoonsful finely chopped parsley	*3 tablespoonsful finely chopped parsley*
3 tablespoonsful finely chopped mint	*3 tablespoonsful finely chopped mint*
½ lb (225g) ricotta cheese	*½ lb ricotta cheese*
2 tablespoonsful grated parmesan cheese	*2 tablespoonsful grated parmesan cheese*

1. Tear the spinach and sorrel leaves away from their stalks and discard the stalks. (If you can't get fresh sorrel, use all spinach.) Wash the leaves, drain and shake off all excess water. Place the leaves in a covered saucepan and cook over a very low heat for about 5-7 minutes. When soft, chop up the leaves with a wooden spoon to almost a purée.
2. Squeeze out all the liquid. Return to a dry pan and add the flour, stirring over a low heat, until the flour is cooked and has thickened the purée a little. Remove from the heat.
3. When the purée is cool, stir in the egg yolks and the double gloucester cheese, mixing and beating well. Whisk the egg whites until stiff and fold into the purée.
4. Preheat the oven to 425°F/220°C (Gas Mark 7). Grease a Swiss roll tin and cut a piece of greaseproof paper the same size as the tin. Butter or oil the paper well, because bits of charred paper sticking to the roulade can be a disaster. Spread the purée evenly over the prepared tin and place in the oven for 15-20 minutes, until the roulade is crisp at the edges and bouncy in the centre. (Stick a knife in the middle; if it comes out clean, the roulade is done.)
5. Make the filling. Infuse the milk by heating it and the infusion ingredients, then leaving it to stand for 10 minutes. Remove herbs.
6. Make a roux with the flour and butter and add to the milk. Mix the parsley and mint with the ricotta cheese, add to the sauce and stir over a low heat. Do not allow it to boil. Keep warm while you are attending to the baked roulade.

7. Sprinkle a fresh piece of greaseproof paper with the parmesan cheese.
8. Smooth the filling over the roulade, but not right to the edges. Nick the edges at each side with a knife about ½ -inch (1.25cm) from the end. Then, lifting the paper beneath, roll up the roulade. Once the first section is tucked under, it will roll easily. Serve at once.

COURGETTES, CARROTS AND TOMATOES

Preparation time: 5 minutes
Cooking time: 40 minutes

IMPERIAL (METRIC)	AMERICAN
4 oz (115g) baby carrots	*¼ lb baby carrots*
1 lb (450g) courgettes	*1 lb zucchini*
½ lb tomatoes	*½ lb tomatoes*
3 tablespoonsful olive oil	*3 tablespoonsful olive oil*
Sea salt and freshly ground black pepper	*Sea salt and freshly ground black pepper*

1. Slice the carrots and boil them for about 5 minutes. Drain. Slice the courgettes and peel and slice the tomatoes.
2. Heat the oil in a pan and cook the courgettes gently for about 10 minutes. Add the carrots and cook for another 10 minutes. Add the tomatoes and cook for a further 15 minutes. Season with salt and pepper.

MELON SALAD

Preparation time: 15 minutes
Cooking time: 10 minutes

IMPERIAL (METRIC)	AMERICAN
6 tablespoonsful orange flower water	*6 tablespoonsful orange flower water*
Juice of 1 large orange	*Juice of 1 large orange*
Juice of 1 large lemon	*Juice of 1 large lemon*
4 oz (115g) caster sugar	*½ cupful superfine sugar*
2 oz (55g) sultanas	*⅓ cupful golden seedless raisins*
1 oz (30g) candied peel	*2 tablespoonsful candied peel*
2 oz (55g) whole hazelnuts	*⅓ cupful whole hazelnuts (filberts)*
½-¾ teaspoonful ground ginger	*½-¾ teaspoonful ground ginger*
1 large melon (3-3½ lb /1.3-1.5kg)	*1 large melon (3-3½ lb)*

1. Place the orange flower water in a small saucepan and reduce, over very low heat, to 2 tablespoonsful. Remove from the heat.
2. Place orange and lemon juice in a pan and add the sugar. Stir over a very low heat until the sugar is dissolved. Add the sultanas, candied peel, hazelnuts and ginger. Bring to the boil and boil fiercely for 2 minutes. Remove from the heat and stir in the orange flower water. Leave to cool.
3. When the syrup is cool, cut the melon in half and remove the seeds. Remove the rind and cut melon flesh into 1-2-inch (2.5-5cm) chunks. Pile the melon into a glass bowl and shortly before serving, pour the fruit and nut syrup over the top.

SUMMER MENU 2

Broad Bean Pâté with Carrot Salad   Muscadet

Tarte aux Courgettes   Rioja
Mange-tout
Sautéed Red Peppers

Vendôme Bleu
Dreux à la Feuille

Raspberries   Sweet Champagne

BROAD BEAN PÂTÉ WITH CARROT SALAD

Preparation time: 15 minutes
Cooking time: 15 minutes
Chilling time: 1 hour

Broad Bean Pâté:

IMPERIAL (METRIC)	AMERICAN
2 lb (900g) broad beans, shelled	*2 lb fava beans, shelled*
6 oz (170g) Quark, fromage frais or *curd cheese*	*¾ cupful fromage frais* or *curd cheese*
1 tablespoonful chopped summer savory or *dill*	*1 tablespoonful chopped summer savory* or *dill*
1 tablespoonful chopped parsley	*1 tablespoonful chopped parsley*
Juice of l lemon	*Juice of 1 lemon*
Sea salt and freshly ground black pepper	*Sea salt and freshly ground black pepper*

Carrot Salad:

IMPERIAL (METRIC)	AMERICAN
1 lb (450g) baby carrots	*1 lb baby carrots*
1 teaspoonful tarragon vinegar	*1 teaspoonful tarragon vinegar*
2 tablespoonsful olive oil	*2 tablespoonsful olive oil*
½ teaspoonful tarragon mustard	*½ teaspoonful tarragon mustard*
Sea salt and freshly ground black pepper	*Sea salt and freshly ground black pepper*

1. Cook the broad (fava) beans in boiling water until they are soft. Drain and purée in a blender. Add all the other ingredients and mix well. Add seasoning to taste, press into an earthenware mould and chill thoroughly, about 1 hour.

2. Cut carrots into julienne strips. Boil until just cooked through. Mix vinegar, oil, mustard and seasoning together. Toss carrots in the dressing while they are still warm. Chill before serving.

TARTE AUX COURGETTES

Preparation time: 15 minutes
Chilling time: 1 hour
Cooking time: 30 minutes
Baking time: 30 minutes

IMPERIAL (METRIC)	AMERICAN
7 oz (200g) plain flour	*1¾ cupsful all-purpose flour*
¾ teaspoonful salt	*¾ teaspoonful salt*
1 egg yolk	*1 egg yolk*
3½ tablespoonsful oil	*3½ tablespoonsful oil*
3-5 tablespoonsful iced water	*3-5 tablespoonsful ice water*

Filling:

¾ lb (340g) courgettes	*¾ lb zucchini*
3½ tablespoonsful rice	*3½ tablespoonsful rice*
1 tablespoonful oil	*1 tablespoonful oil*
½ onion, finely chopped	*½ onion, minced*
1 clove garlic, finely chopped	*1 clove garlic, minced*
2 oz (55g) grated gruyère cheese	*½ cupful grated unprocessed*
1 egg	*gruyère cheese*
Sea salt and freshly ground black	*1 egg*
pepper	*Sea salt and freshly ground black*
	pepper

Topping:

1 oz (30g) grated gruyère cheese	*¼ cupful grated unprocessed*
1 tablespoonful oil	*gruyère cheese*
	1 tablespoonful oil

1. Make the pastry. Sift the flour into a bowl, make a well in the centre, drop the salt, egg yolk, oil and 3 tablespoonsful water into the well and mix together with the fingertips until the salt has dissolved. Work in the flour until the mixture resembles fine breadcrumbs, then press the dough firmly together. If it doesn't hold together, sprinkle with another tablespoon or two of water. Gather the dough into a ball, wrap with cling film and refrigerate for 1 hour.

2. Preheat the oven to 400°F/200°C (Gas Mark 6). Roll out the dough, line a tart with the pastry and bake blind for about 15 minutes.

3. Cut the courgettes (zucchini) into ½-inch (1.25cm) slices. Cook in boiling water for about 10 minutes. Drain.

4. Cook the rice in boiling water until tender, about 12 minutes. Drain.

5. Heat the oil in a pan, add the onion and cook for about 5 minutes or until soft. Add the garlic and cook for another minute.

6. Mash the courgettes with a fork and add the rice, onion, garlic, grated cheese, egg and salt and pepper to taste. Spread on the baked tart shell. Sprinkle with the remaining grated cheese and oil. Bake for 25-30 minutes until the filling is set and the top is lightly browned.

SAUTÉED RED PEPPERS

Preparation time: 5 minutes
Cooking time: 7 minutes

IMPERIAL (METRIC)
4 red peppers
2 tablespoonsful olive oil
1 tablespoonful walnut oil
1 tablespoonful green peppercorns
*Sea salt and freshly ground black
   pepper*

AMERICAN
4 red peppers
2 tablespoonsful olive oil
1 tablespoonful walnut oil
1 tablespoonful green peppercorns
*Sea salt and freshly ground black
   pepper*

1. Cut the tops off the peppers and deseed. Cut the flesh into strips.
2. Heat the olive oil in a frying pan, add the peppers and cook for about 5 minutes. Add the walnut oil and peppercorns and cook for a further 2 minutes. Season to taste. Serve hot.

MANGE-TOUT

Boil briefly for about 2 minutes, or steam for 4 minutes. The fresh taste of mange-tout is the perfect alternative to a green salad.

RASPBERRIES

Fresh raspberries at the peak of their season need nothing added to them except a little caster sugar and perhaps a splash of red wine in which they marinate for about an hour before serving.

SUMMER MENU 3

Stuffed Globe Artichokes	Fendant
Avocado Soufflé	Chevalier-Montrachet
Succotash	
New Potatoes with Mint (See page 61)	
Mixed Green Salad (See page 94)	
Coulommiers	
Dolcelatte	
Wensleydale	
The Strawberry Alternative	

STUFED GLOBE ARTICHOKES

Preparation time: 10 minutes
Cooking time: 40 minutes
Chilling time: 2 hours

IMPERIAL (METRIC)
6-8 globe artichokes
1 14-oz (395g) tin artichoke bottoms
Zest and juice of 1 lemon
1 clove garlic, crushed
¼ pint (150ml) soured cream
Sea salt and freshly ground black pepper

AMERICAN
6-8 globe artichokes
1 14-oz can artichoke bottoms
Zest and juice of 1 lemon
1 clove garlic, crushed
⅔ cupful sour cream
Sea salt and freshly ground black pepper

1. Trim the bottoms and snip the points of the artichoke leaves off. Boil the artichokes for 30-40 minutes, or until they are tender. Drain.
2. Pull out the centre bunch of leaves in each artichoke and scrape away the edible part of the leaves (there is more than you think). Place in a bowl. Cut out the chokes with a knife, leaving a container for the stuffing, the base of which is the artichoke bottom.
3. Drain the tinned artichoke bottoms and dice. Add these to the bowl with the edible scrapings of the leaves and add the rest of the ingredients. Mix well.
4. Pile the stuffing mixture into the artichokes. Chill for about 2 hours before serving.

AVOCADO SOUFFLÉ

Preparation time: 15 minutes
Baking time: 25 minutes

IMPERIAL (METRIC)
3 ripe avocados
½ pint (300ml) single cream
6 eggs, separated
Sea salt and freshly ground black
    pepper

AMERICAN
3 ripe avocados
1¼ cupsful light cream
6 eggs, separated
Sea salt and freshly ground black
    pepper

1. Peel and stone the avocados. Cut the flesh into slices and place in a bowl with the cream and egg yolks. Mix well.
2. Preheat the oven to 400°F/200°C (Gas Mark 6). Whisk the egg whites until stiff. Fold into the avocado mixture. Season.
3. Generously butter a large soufflé dish. Pour in the avocado mixture and bake for about 20-25 minutes, or until the top is well-risen. The centre should still be runny. Each person should be served a crisp part and a runny part, which acts as a sauce.

SUCCOTASH

Preparation time: 10 minutes
Cooking time: 15 minutes

IMPERIAL (METRIC)
1 lb (450g) corn, cut from the cob
    (about 6 ears)
1 lb (450g) broad beans
2 oz (55g) butter
Sea salt and freshly ground black
    pepper

AMERICAN
1 lb corn, cut from the cob (about 6
    ears)
1 lb fava beans
4 tablespoonsful butter
Sea salt and freshly ground black
    pepper

1. Cut the corn from the cobs and boil in a little salted water until tender, about 4 minutes.
2. Cook the broad (fava) beans until tender in boiling, salted water. (Depending on their age, it will take up to 10 minutes. If too old, their outer skins will have to be peeled away.)
3. Mix the two vegetables together and add the butter and salt and pepper to taste. Mix well. Serve.

THE STRAWBERRY ALTERNATIVE

Hull the strawberries and place in a large glass bowl. Squeeze the juice of 2 lemons over them, then pour over half a bottle of red wine. Liberally sprinkle with caster sugar and leave them to marinate for several hours before serving. Do not use cream.

SUMMER MENU 4
(Illustrated between pages 120 and 121.)

Summer Crudités with Mayonnaise	**Meursault**
Chilled Cucumber and Grapefruit Soup	**Margaux**
Corn Fritters	
Courgettes in Sweet and Sour Sauce	
Pommes de Terre Sablées	
Mixed Green Salad (See page 94)	
Rollot	
Parfait	
Bleu de Gex	
Strawberry and Pineapple Salad	**Eau de Vie**

SUMMER CRUDITÉS WITH MAYONNAISE

Preparation time: 20 minutes

Any selection of summer vegetables, freshly picked, sliced and cut delicately is a delightful and stimulating way of beginning a meal. When accompanied with home-made mayonnaise to dip the vegetables into, it is sublime. Garlic lovers may add 2-3 crushed cloves of garlic to the mayonnaise. (See page 19.)

CHILLED CUCUMBER AND GRAPEFRUIT SOUP

Preparation time: 15 minutes
Standing time: 1 hour
Chilling time: 2 hours

IMPERIAL (METRIC)	AMERICAN
2 large cucumbers	*2 large cucumbers*
2 grapefruits (pink if possible)	*2 grapefruits (pink if possible)*
½ pint (300ml) natural yogurt	*1¼ cupsful plain yogurt*
Sea salt and white pepper	*Sea salt and white pepper*
2 tablespoonsful chopped fresh mint	*2 tablespoonsful chopped fresh mint*

1. Cut the cucumbers in half lengthways. If they have large seeds, scoop them out and discard. Otherwise, grate everything, skins and all, into a bowl. Sprinkle with ½ teaspoonful salt and leave for 1 hour.
2. Extract all the flesh from the grapefruit and put into a blender container, discarding all skin, pips and pith. Add the undrained cucumbers and blend at a high speed.
3. Add the yogurt and a little white pepper. Pour into a bowl and sprinkle with mint. Chill and serve with ice cubes floating on the surface.

CORN FRITTERS

Preparation time: 10 minutes
Cooking time: 15 minutes

IMPERIAL (METRIC)	AMERICAN
½ lb (225g) corn, cut from the cob (about 3 ears)	*½ lb corn, cut from the cob (about 3 ears)*
4 tablespoonsful double cream	*4 tablespoonsful heavy cream*
2 tablespoonsful flour	*2 tablespoonful flour*
½ teaspoonsful baking powder	*½ teaspoonful baking powder*
Sea salt and freshly ground black pepper	*Sea salt and freshly ground black pepper*
½ teaspoonful sugar	*½ teaspoonful sugar*
Butter for frying	*Butter for frying*

1. Cut the corn from the cob with a sharp knife. Place the corn and any juice into a bowl and add the cream, flour, baking powder, salt, pepper and sugar and mix well.
2. Heat a small piece of butter in a griddle or shallow frying pan. Drop spoonsful of the corn mixture into the pan and flatten them with a palette knife into the shape of small, flat cakes. Fry until golden brown, about 4 minutes on each side. Cook in batches if necessary and keep warm.

COURGETTES IN SWEET AND SOUR SAUCE

Preparation time: 10 minutes
Cooking time: 15 minutes

IMPERIAL (METRIC)	AMERICAN
1½ lb (680g) courgettes	*1½ lb zucchini*
1 tablespoonful olive oil	*1 tablespoonful olive oil*
1 large onion, finely chopped	*1 large onion, minced*
1 tablesponful malt vinegar	*1 tablespoonful malt vinegar*
1 tablespoonful soya sauce	*1 tablespoonful soy sauce*
1 tablespoonful each: sultanas and almonds	*1 tablespoonful each: golden seedless raisins and almonds*
1 teaspoonful crushed cloves	*1 teaspoonful crushed cloves*
2 tablespoonsful honey	*2 tablespoonsful honey*
1 tablespoonful grated bitter chocolate	*1 tablespoonful grated bitter chocolate*
Sea salt and freshly ground black pepper	*Sea salt and freshly ground black pepper*

1. Cut unpared courgettes (zucchini) into ½-inch (1.25cm) slices.
2. Heat the oil in a large saucepan and cook the onion until soft, about 5 minutes. Add the courgettes. Stir well. Add the rest of the ingredients, stir and cook for a further 10 minutes.

POMMES DE TERRE SABLÉES (Sauté Potatoes with Breadcrumbs)

Preparation time: 10 minutes
Cooking time: 30 minutes

IMPERIAL (METRIC)	AMERICAN
2 lb (900g) small new potatoes	*2 lb small new potatoes*
4 oz (115g) butter	*½ cupful (1 stick) butter*
Sea salt and freshly ground black pepper to taste	*Sea salt and freshly ground black pepper to taste*
3 tablespoonful breadcrumbs	*3 tablespoonful bread crumbs*

1. Scrub the potatoes. Melt the butter in a pan large enough to hold the potatoes snugly in one layer. Cook, uncovered over a gentle heat so that the butter does not burn, turning them from time to time so that they brown on all sides, about 25 minutes.
2. Sprinkle with the breadcrumbs and shake the pan. Cook the potatoes for a further 3 minutes with the lid on the pan. Season to taste.

STRAWBERRY AND PINEAPPLE SALAD

Preparation time: 15 minutes

IMPERIAL (METRIC)	AMERICAN
1 lb (450g) strawberries	*1 quart strawberries*
1 ripe pineapple	*1 ripe pineapple*
1 tablespoonful caster sugar	*1 tablespoonful superfine sugar*
Juice of 1 lemon	*Juice of 1 lemon*
½ pint (300ml) double cream	*1¼ cupsful heavy cream*
Grated zest and juice of 1 orange	*Grated zest and juice of 1 orange*

1. Cut the strawberries in half if they are large. Cut the rind off the pineapple and discard. Cut the pineapple flesh into small chunks.
2. Mix the strawberries and pineapple together in a glass bowl. Stir in the sugar and lemon juice.
3. Whip the cream until stiff. Stir in the orange zest and juice. Serve the cream separately with the salad.

SUMMER MENU 5

Chilled Avocado Soup	Chablis
Salsify Soufflé	Beaune
Colcannon	
French Beans	
Green Salad (See page 30)	
Cantal	
Sancerre	
Brie	
Red, White and Blackcurrants	Monbazillac

CHILLED AVOCADO SOUP

Preparation time: 15 minutes
Chilling time: 2 hours

IMPERIAL (METRIC)	AMERICAN
3 ripe avocados	*3 ripe avocados*
8 fl oz (240ml) single cream	*1 cupful light cream*
2½ fl oz (75ml) sherry	*⅓ cupful sherry*
1¾ pints (1 litre) vegetable stock	*1 quart vegetable stock*
Dash of tabasco sauce	*Dash of tabasco sauce*
Sea salt and freshly ground black pepper	*Sea salt and freshly ground black pepper*
2 tablespoonsful chopped chives	*2 tablespoonsful chopped chives*

1. Cut the avocados in half and remove stones. Scoop the flesh into a blender container. Add the cream and sherry. Blend to a smooth purée. Add the vegetable stock, tabasco and seasoning. Pour into a tureen and chill for about 2 hours. Sprinkle with chives before serving.

Opposite: Gruyère Salad Roulade (page 130) *and* Marinated Mushrooms (page 131).
Overleaf: Summer Menu 4 (page 117 to 119).
Opposite page 121: Gooseberry Fool (page 124).

SALSIFY SOUFFLÉ

Preparation time: 10 minutes
Baking time: 25 minutes

IMPERIAL (METRIC)
1 14-oz (395g) tin salsify
6 eggs, separated
½ pint (300ml) single cream
Sea salt and freshly ground black
   pepper

AMERICAN
1 14-oz can salsify (oyster plant)
6 eggs, separated
1¼ cupsful light cream
Sea salt and freshly ground black
   pepper

1. Drain and mash the salsify well. Place into a bowl with the egg yolks and cream and mix thoroughly. Season to taste.
2. Preheat the oven to 400°F/200°C (Gas Mark 6).
3. Whisk the egg whites until stiff and fold into the salsify mixture. Butter a 9 × 3½-inch (22.5 × 9 cm) soufflé dish generously. Pour the mixture into the soufflé dish and bake for 20-25 minutes. The top should be well-risen and crisp and some of the inside should still be runny.

COLCANNON

Preparation time: 10 minutes
Cooking time: 30 minutes

IMPERIAL (METRIC)
1 lb (450g) spring greens or kale
2 bunches spring onions
¼ pint (150ml) milk
1½ lb (680g) potatoes
3 oz (85g) butter
Sea salt and freshly ground black
   pepper
Melted butter to serve

AMERICAN
1 lb spring greens or kale
2 bunches scallions
⅔ cupful milk
1½ lb potatoes
6 tablespoonsful butter
Sea salt and freshly ground black
   pepper
Melted butter to serve

1. Wash the greens or kale and cut into strips. Cook in a little boiling salted water until tender, about 3-5 minutes. Drain well.
2. Chop the spring onions (scallions) and cook in the milk for a few minutes.
3. Boil the potatoes until tender. Drain, then mash them. Stir in the greens, milk and onions. Add the butter, salt and pepper to taste and beat the mixture so it has plenty of air in it. Serve with extra butter melted on top.

RED, WHITE AND BLACKCURRANTS

Take the currants off their stalks, top and tail them and place each colour in a separate bowl. Sprinkle with a little caster sugar. Just before serving, arrange the whitecurrants in a pile in the centre of a serving dish, make a ring around them with the blackcurrants, and place the redcurrants around the edge of the dish. Serve with whipped cream if you wish, but on their own, currants are the best summer dessert ever.

SUMMER MENU 6

Cream of Green Pea Soup	Muscadet
Oeufs durs Soubise	Primeur-Lichine
Mange-tout	
New Potatoes with Mint (See page 61)	
Cucumber and Chive Salad	
Tomme au Marc	
Tamié	
Blue Vinny	
	Muscat de
Gooseberry Fool	Beaumes-de-Venise

CREAM OF GREEN PEA SOUP

Preparation time: 15 minutes
Cooking time: 20 minutes

IMPERIAL (METRIC)
1 lb (450g) fresh peas in their pods
1 Cos or Density lettuce
2 pints (1.2 litres) water
4 oz (115g) butter
Sea salt and freshly ground black
   pepper
½ pint (300ml) single cream
½ teaspoonful sugar (optional)

AMERICAN
1 lb fresh peas in their pods
1 leaf lettuce
5 cupsful water
½ cupful (1 stick) butter
Sea salt and freshly ground black
   pepper
1¼ cupsful light cream
½ teaspoonful sugar (optional)

1. Shell the peas, reserving the pods. Take the outer leaves from the lettuce and cook with the pea pods in the measured water for 10 minutes. Cool. Blend to a purée and put through a sieve. Discard the pulp. Set the stock aside.

2. Simmer the peas and lettuce heart in the butter for 10 minutes in a pan with a tight-fitting lid. Add the hot stock from the pods, season and continue to cook until the peas are tender. Cool. Blend to a purée, adding more vegetable stock if there is not enough liquid.

3. Return to the pan and reheat, adding the cream at the last moment. Some palates may need a bit of sugar added as well.

OEUFS DURS SOUBISE (Egg and Onion Gratin)

Preparation time: 5 minutes
Cooking time: 20 minutes
Baking time: 10 minutes

IMPERIAL (METRIC)
6-8 eggs
2 oz (55g) butter
1½ lb (680g) onions, diced
1 tablespoonful flour
¾ pint (450ml) milk
1 teaspoonful Dijon mustard
Sea salt and freshly ground black
 pepper
2 tablespoonsful breadcrumbs

AMERICAN
6-8 eggs
4 tablespoonsful butter
1½ lb onions, diced
1 tablespoonful flour
2 cupsful milk
1 teaspoonful Dijon mustard
Sea salt and freshly ground black
 pepper
2 tablespoonsful bread crumbs

1. Hard-boil the eggs, peel and set aside.
2. Melt the butter in a saucepan and cook the onions until they are soft, about 5-10 minutes. Sprinkle with flour and slowly add the milk to make a thick sauce. Stir in the mustard and seasoning.
3. Preheat the oven to 400°F/200°C (Gas Mark 6).
4. Butter a large, shallow ovenproof dish. Halve the eggs and arrange in the dish in a circular pattern. Cover with the onion sauce and sprinkle the breadcrumbs on top. Pop into the oven for 10 minutes, until the top is brown and crisp.

CUCUMBER AND CHIVE SALAD

Preparation time: 10 minutes
Standing time: 1 hour
Chilling time: 1 hour

IMPERIAL (METRIC)
1 large cucumber
1 teaspoonful tarragon vinegar
1 teaspoonful olive oil
½ teaspoonful sugar
2 tablespoonsful soured cream
Sea salt and freshly ground black
 pepper
3 tablespoonsful chopped chives

AMERICAN
1 large cucumber
1 teaspoonful tarragon vinegar
1 teaspoonful olive oil
½ teaspoonful sugar
2 tablespoonsful sour cream
Sea salt and freshly ground black
 pepper
3 tablespoonsful chopped chives

1. Slice the cucumber thinly. Sprinkle with a little salt and leave for 1 hour.
2. Mix all the other ingredients together, except for the chives.
3. Rinse the cucumber under a cold tap, drain and pat dry. Place the cucumber in a bowl, pour the dressing over and sprinkle with chives. Chill before serving, about 1 hour.

GOOSEBERRY FOOL

(Illustrated opposite page 121.)
Cooking time: 10 minutes
Preparation time: 5 minutes

IMPERIAL (METRIC)	AMERICAN
1½ lb (680g) gooseberries	*1½ lb gooseberries*
1 tablespoonful caster sugar	*1 tablespoonful superfine sugar*
¼ pint (150ml) double cream	*⅔ cupful heavy cream*

1. Place the gooseberries in a pan with the sugar and let them cook by steaming in their own juices over a very low heat for about 10 minutes. Remove from the heat and leave to cool.
2. Whip the cream until stiff and mix with the gooseberries. Serve in individual glasses.

Note: Gooseberries are so sensational in flavour, they need little cream and little sugar. Their sharpness should be enjoyed, for the season for them is *so* short.

SUMMER MENU 7

Chilled Tomato and Red Pepper Soup	Montrachet
Charlotte de Pois	Haut-Bailly
Baked Spiced Potatoes	
Curly Endive Salad	
Beenleigh Blue	
Cotherstone	
Cheddar	
Fried Bread Apple Pie	Calvados

CHILLED TOMATO AND RED PEPPER SOUP

Preparation time: 15 minutes
Cooking time: 25 minutes
Chilling time: 2 hours

IMPERIAL (METRIC)	AMERICAN
1½ lb (680g) tomatoes	*1½ lb tomatoes*
2 red peppers	*2 red peppers*
2 tablespoonsful olive oil	*2 tablespoonsful olive oil*
½ pint (300ml) vegetable stock	*1¼ cupsful vegetable stock*
½ pint (300ml) red wine	*1¼ cupsful red wine*
1 tablespoonful wine vinegar	*1 tablespoonful wine vinegar*
Sea salt and freshly ground black pepper	*Sea salt and freshly ground black pepper*
1 small red pepper to garnish	*1 small red pepper to garnish*
2 peeled tomatoes to garnish	*2 peeled tomatoes to garnish*

1. Do not peel tomatoes. Cut them in half and cook with a pinch of salt in a pan with a tight-fitting lid for about 10 minutes. Cool. Sieve the tomatoes and discard the pulp.
2. Deseed the peppers and slice them. Place the olive oil in another saucepan and cook the peppers for a few minutes. Add the vegetable stock and continue to cook for another 10 minutes. Cool, then pop in the blender and liquidize.
3. Add the wine and tomato juice to the peppers with the wine vinegar, salt and pepper. Reheat and let it boil for a moment or two. Taste and check seasoning. Cool. Refrigerate for about 2 hours before serving.
4. Deseed and slice the red pepper. Slice the tomatoes. Float on top of the soup to serve.

CHARLOTTE DE POIS

Preparation time: 15 minutes
Cooking time: 25 minutes
Baking time: 15 minutes

IMPERIAL (METRIC)	AMERICAN
2 lb (900g) garden peas	*2 lb garden peas*
½ pint (300ml) single cream	*1¼ cupsful light cream*
Sea salt and freshly ground black pepper	*Sea salt and freshly ground black pepper*
Pinch of sugar	*Pinch of sugar*

Omelettes:

4 oz (115g) pistachio nuts	*1 cupful pistachio nuts*
6 eggs	*6 eggs*
Sea salt and freshly ground black pepper	*Sea salt and freshly ground black pepper*
3 tablespoonsful single cream	*3 tablespoonsful light cream*
Pinch of nutmeg	*Pinch of nutmeg*
Butter for the omelettes	*Butter for the omelettes*

1. Shell peas and cook in boiling salted water until tender. Drain, reserving 2 tablespoonsful water. When the peas are cool, place them in a blender container with the cream, reserved water, seasoning and a pinch of sugar. Blend to a thin purée.

2. Shell the pistachio nuts. Beat the eggs together with the nuts, seasoning, cream and nutmeg.

3. Divide the omelette mixture into thirds. Place a little butter in a frying pan and make 3 omelettes, making sure each has its quota of pistachio nuts. (Using a pan which is the same size as the soufflé dish you will make the charlotte in will ensure that the omelettes are the right size.)

4. Preheat the oven to 425°F/220°C (Gas Mark 7). Assemble the charlotte. Place one omelette into a well-buttered soufflé dish and pour some pea purée over the omelette. Continue with the rest of the omelettes and purée, ending with the purée. Bake for 15 minutes.

BAKED SPICED POTATOES

Preparation time: 10 minutes
Cooking time: 15 minutes
Baking time: 30 minutes

IMPERIAL (METRIC)	AMERICAN
2 teaspoonsful sunflower oil	*2 teaspoonsful sunflower oil*
5 crushed bay leaves	*5 crushed bay leaves*
1 teaspoonful each: turmeric, garam masala and chilli powder	*1 teaspoonful each: turmeric, garam masala and chili powder*
1 teaspoonful muscovado sugar	*1 teaspoonful dark brown sugar*
4 cloves garlic, crushed	*4 cloves garlic, crushed*
Sea salt and freshly ground black pepper	*Sea salt and freshly ground black pepper*
1 pint (600ml) natural yogurt	*2½ cupsful plain yogurt*
6-8 large potatoes	*6-8 large potatoes*
Handful of chopped coriander leaves	*Handful of chopped cilantro*

1. Heat the oil and fry the bay leaves and other spices for a few moments, then stir in the sugar and garlic. Add salt and pepper, then mix with the yogurt.
2. Preheat the oven to 400°F/200°C (Gas Mark 6).
3. Peel the potatoes and parboil them, whole, for about 12 minutes. Drain and prick them all over with a fork. Place the spiced yogurt mixture in an ovenproof dish and roll the potatoes around in it, making sure all sides are covered.
4. Bake the potatoes for about 30 minutes. Sprinkle with coriander before serving.

CURLY ENDIVE SALAD

Marinating time: 1 hour
Preparation time: 5 minutes

IMPERIAL (METRIC)	AMERICAN
1 onion, thinly sliced	*1 onion, thinly sliced*
1 tablespoonful raspberry vinegar	*1 tablespoonful raspberry vinegar*
Sea salt and freshly ground black pepper	*Sea salt and freshly ground black pepper*
2 tablespoonsful walnut oil	*2 tablespoonsful walnut oil*
1 curly endive	*1 head chicory*

1. Place the sliced onion in a salad bowl with the raspberry vinegar, salt and pepper and leave to marinate for 1 hour.
2. Add the walnut oil and mix well.
3. Wash the endive (chicory) and tear into small pieces. Toss well with the ingredients in the salad bowl before serving.

FRIED BREAD APPLE PIE

Preparation time: 10 minutes
Cooking time: 15 minutes
Baking time: 15 minutes

IMPERIAL (METRIC)	AMERICAN
1 small wholemeal loaf	*1 small wholewheat bread*
6 oz (170g) butter	*¾ cupful butter*
1½ lb (680g) apples, peeled, cored and sliced	*1½ lb apples, pared, cored and sliced*
4 tablespoonsful muscovado sugar	*4 tablespoonsful dark brown sugar*
Juice of 1 lemon	*Juice of 1 lemon*
1 teaspoonful ground cinnamon	*1 teaspoonful ground cinnamon*
Whipped cream to serve	*Whipped cream to serve*

1. Cut the loaf into fingers and fry in some of the butter until crisp and golden. Line a pie dish with half of the bread.
2. Fry the apple slices in more of the butter with 3 tablespoonsful of the sugar, lemon juice and cinnamon until it becomes a sticky goo. Place the apple mixture on top of the bread fingers.
3. Preheat the oven to 400°F/200°C (Gas Mark 6).
4. Place the remaining fried bread on top of the apple mixture. Sprinkle with more sugar and dot with the remaining butter. Bake for 15 minutes, or until crisp on top. Serve with whipped cream.

SUMMER MENU 8

Chilled Beetroot and Ginger Soup   Chablis

Gruyère Salad Roulade   Chianti
Marinated Mushrooms
Potato Salad

Swaledale
Caboc
Cheddar

Fraises à la Crème   Sweet Champagne

CHILLED BEETROOT AND GINGER SOUP

Preparation time:	10 minutes
Baking time:	3 hours
Chilling time:	2 hours

IMPERIAL (METRIC)	AMERICAN
1 lb (450g) raw beetroot	*1 lb raw beets*
½ cabbage, thinly sliced	*½ cabbage, thinly sliced*
6 cloves garlic, sliced	*6 cloves garlic, sliced*
2 oz (55g) grated root ginger	*¾ cupful grated ginger root*
Sea salt and freshly ground black pepper	*Sea salt and freshly ground black pepper*
Soured cream to serve	*Sour cream to serve*
Raw, grated beetroot to garnish	*Raw, grated beets to garnish*

1. Preheat the oven to 350°F/180°F (Gas Mark 4).
2. Peel and slice the beetroot and place in a large casserole dish, interleaved with the cabbage, garlic and ginger. Sprinkle the vegetables with salt and pepper and cover with enough boiling water to come 2 inches (5cm) above the vegetables.
3. Cover the casserole and bake for 2½-3 hours.
4. Remove from the oven and strain all the liquid into a bowl or tureen. (The liquid should be clear and red with a pungent and delicious flavour). Discard the vegetables as all of their goodness has gone into the stock. Chill for about 2 hours. Serve with soured cream and a little raw grated beetroot floating on the top.

GRUYÈRE SALAD ROULADE

(Illustrated opposite page 120.)

Preparation time: 15 minutes
Baking time: 15 minutes

IMPERIAL (METRIC)	AMERICAN
2 tablespoonsful grated parmesan cheese	2 tablespoonsful grated parmesan cheese
2 oz (55g) fresh wholemeal breadcrumbs	1 cupful fresh wholewheat bread crumbs
6 oz (170g) grated gruyère cheese	1½ cupsful grated unprocessed gruyère cheese
4 eggs, separated	4 eggs, separated
¼ pint (150ml) single cream	⅔ cupful light cream
Sea salt and freshly ground black pepper	Sea salt and freshly ground black pepper
2-3 pinches cayenne pepper	2-3 pinches cayenne pepper
2 tablespoonsful warm water	2 tablespoonsful warm water
4-5 tablespoonsful mayonnaise	4-5 tablespoonsful mayonnaise
¼-½ crisp lettuce, shredded	¼-½ crisp lettuce, shredded
2-3 tomatoes, finely sliced	2-3 tomatoes, finely sliced
1 oz (30g) mushrooms, finely sliced	½ cupful finely sliced mushrooms
1 tablespoonful fresh chives, parsley or mint, chopped	1 tablespoonful fresh chives, parsley or mint, chopped
Bunch of watercress to garnish	Bunch of watercress to garnish

1. Preheat the oven to 400°F/200°C (Gas Mark 6). Line a Swiss roll tin with a piece of greaseproof paper and sprinkle with half the parmesan cheese.
2. Mix the breadcrumbs and gruyère cheese together in a bowl. Add the egg yolks, cream, salt, pepper and cayenne pepper. Stir in the water.
3. Whisk egg whites until stiff. Fold into the cheese mixture. Pour into the baking tin and bake for 10-15 minutes, until firm and springy to the touch. Remove from the oven and let cool.
4. Sprinkle another piece of greaseproof paper with the rest of the parmesan cheese and turn the cheese roulade onto the paper. Peel off the paper on top and spread the roulade with mayonnaise, then sprinkle with the lettuce, tomatoes, mushrooms and herbs. Roll up loosely, but firmly.
5. Transfer to a serving dish, garnish with watercress and serve in slices.

MARINATED MUSHROOMS
(Illustrated opposite page 120.)
Preparation time: 10 minutes
Cooking time: 3 minutes
Marinating time: 4 hours

IMPERIAL (METRIC)	AMERICAN
½ lb (225g) small whole mushrooms	*½ lb small whole mushrooms*
5 tablespoonsful olive oil	*5 tablespoonsful olive oil*
Juice of 1 lemon	*Juice of 1 lemon*
3 cloves garlic, crushed	*3 cloves garlic, crushed*
2 onions, sliced into rings	*2 onions, sliced into rings*
1 teaspoonful crushed coriander seeds	*1 teaspoonful crushed coriander seeds*
Sea salt and freshly ground black pepper	*Sea salt and freshly ground black pepper*
Handful of fresh mint and parsley	*Handful of fresh mint and parsley*

1. Slice the mushrooms thinly, including their stems, and arrange in a shallow serving dish.
2. Place all the other ingredients except for the mint and parsley in a pan and bring to the boil. Simmer for 2-3 minutes, then pour over the mushrooms. Sprinkle with the mint and parsley and marinate for about 4 hours.

POTATO SALAD
Preparation time: Cooking the potatoes, plus 15 minutes
Cooling time: 1 hour

IMPERIAL (METRIC)	AMERICAN
1½ lb (680g) cooked new potatoes	*1½ lb cooked new potatoes*
3 tablespoonsful olive oil	*3 tablespoonsful olive oil*
1 tablespoonful cider vinegar	*1 tablespoonful cider vinegar*
2 cloves garlic, crushed	*2 cloves garlic, crushed*
Sea salt and freshly ground black pepper	*Sea salt and freshly ground black pepper*
¼ pint (150ml) mayonnaise	*⅔ cupful mayonnaise*
4-5 tablespoonsful chopped chives	*4-5 tablespoonsful chopped chives*

1. Dice the potatoes. Mix the oil, vinegar, garlic and seasoning together in a large salad bowl. Add the potatoes while still warm, if possible and mix well so that they soak up the vinaigrette.
2. When cold, add the mayonnaise and chives. Turn the salad in the dressing to ensure that all the potato pieces are well-covered.

FRAISES À LA CRÈME (Strawberries in Liqueur and Cream)

Preparation time: 10 minutes
Standing time: 3 hours

IMPERIAL (METRIC)
1 lb (450g) whole fresh strawberries
4 tablespoonsful caster sugar
4 tablespoonsful orange curaçao or
  cherry brandy
½ pint (300ml) double cream
2 crisp macaroons

AMERICAN
1 quart whole fresh strawberries
4 tablespoonsful superfine sugar
4 tablespoonsful orange curaçao or
  cherry brandy
1¼ cupsful heavy cream
2 crisp macaroons

1. Hull the strawberries. Place them in a large glass bowl and sprinkle with the sugar. Cover and leave in a cool place for 1 hour.
2. Pour the liqueur over the strawberries, cover and leave for a further 2 hours.
3. Whip the cream until stiff and crumble the macaroons into it. Fold the cream into the strawberries just before serving.

SUMMER MENU 9

Profiteroles au Gruyère	Verdicchio dei Castelli di Jesi
Avocado Purée with Broad Beans Nepal Spiced Eggs Rice Salad Mixed Green Salad (See page 94)	Venegazzu'
Stilton from the Vale of Belvoir Cheddar	
Fraises à l'Orange	Sweet Champagne

PROFITEROLES AU GRUYÈRE

Preparation time:	20 minutes
Cooking time:	10 minutes
Baking time:	30 minutes

IMPERIAL (METRIC)
Profiteroles:
5 oz (140g) plain flour
1 teaspoonful sea salt
½ teaspoonful cayenne pepper
½ pint (300ml) water
4 oz (115g) butter
3 eggs
4 oz (115g) grated gruyère cheese

Filling:
1 lb /450g) frozen peas
Handful of mint leaves, chopped
4 tablespoonsful single cream
Sea salt and freshly ground black
  pepper
Pinch of nutmeg
6-8 fl oz (180-240ml) mayonnaise
Lettuce, watercress and tomatoes to
  garnish

AMERICAN

1¼ cupsful all-purpose flour
1 teaspoonful sea salt
½ teaspoonful cayenne pepper
1¼ cupsful water
½ cupful (1 stick) butter
3 eggs
1 cupful grated unprocessed gruyère
  cheese

1 lb frozen peas
Handful of mint leaves, chopped
4 tablespoonsful light cream
Sea salt and freshly ground black
  pepper
Pinch of nutmeg
¾-1 cupful mayonnaise
Lettuce, watercress and tomatoes to
  garnish

1. Sift the flour, salt and cayenne pepper into a bowl. Place the water and butter in a heavy saucepan and boil until the butter is melted. Tip in the flour all at once and beat with

a wooden spoon until smooth. Continue beating until the mixture leaves the sides of the pan. Remove from the heat.

2. Preheat the oven to 425°F/220°C (Gas Mark 7).

3. Beat the eggs into the flour mixture one at a time, beating thoroughly between each addition, until the mixture is smooth and glossy. Beat in all but 4 tablespoonsful of the cheese.

4. Grease a large baking tray and drop tablespoonsful of the mixture on the tray leaving space between them. Sprinkle with the reserved cheese. Bake in the centre of the oven for 25-30 minutes, or until well puffed up and golden brown. Remove from the oven and cool on a wire rack.

5. Meanwhile, make the filling. Cook the peas until tender, drain and place in a blender container with the mint and cream. Blend to a thick purée. Season well with salt, pepper and nutmeg. Transfer to a bowl and mix in the mayonnaise.

6. When the profiteroles are cold, cut the tops off and spoon in the filling. Replace the lids. Serve the profiteroles on a large platter on a bed of lettuce leaves, decorated with the watercress and sliced tomatoes.

AVOCADO PURÉE WITH BROAD BEANS

Preparation time: 15 minutes
Cooking time: 10 minutes

IMPERIAL (METRIC)	AMERICAN
Avocado Purée:	
4 ripe avocados	*4 ripe avocados*
Juice of 1 lemon	*Juice of 1 lemon*
¼ pint (150ml) natural yogurt	*⅔ cupful plain yogurt*
¼ pint (150ml) soured cream	*⅔ cupful sour cream*
2 tablespoonsful olive oil	*2 tablespoonsful olive oil*
Dash of tabasco sauce	*Dash of tabasco sauce*
Sea salt and freshly ground black pepper	*Sea salt and freshly ground black pepper*
Broad Beans:	
1 lb (450g) broad beans, shelled	*1 lb fava beans, shelled*
2 teaspoonsful lemon juice	*2 teaspoonsful lemon juice*
2 tablespoonsful olive oil	*2 tablespoonsful olive oil*
Sea salt and freshly ground black pepper	*Sea salt and freshly ground black pepper*
2 tablespoonsful grated carrot to garnish	*2 tablespoonsful grated carrot to garnish*

1. Cut the avocados in half and remove the stones. Scoop out the flesh and place in a blender container with the rest of the purée ingredients. Blend until smooth.

2. Meanwhile, cook the beans until they are tender. While they are still warm, toss them with the lemon juice, olive oil and seasoning.

3. Pile the avocado purée around the sides of a large serving dish, leaving a well in the centre. Fill the hollow with the beans and sprinkle the grated carrot over the beans.

NEPAL SPICED EGGS

Preparation time: 10 minutes
Cooking time: 4 minutes

IMPERIAL (METRIC)	AMERICAN
1 tablespoonful butter	*1 tablespoonful butter,*
1 teaspoonful each: crushed cardamom, caraway and sesame seeds, cumin and paprika	*1 teaspoonful each: crushed cardamom, caraway and sesame seeds, cumin and paprika*
½ pint (300ml) natural yogurt	*1¼ cupsful plain yogurt*
Juice of 1 lemon	*Juice of 1 lemon*
Handful of chopped coriander leaves	*Handful of chopped cilantro*
6-8 hard-boiled eggs	*6-8 hard-cooked eggs*

1. Heat the butter in a saucepan. Add the crushed spices and cook, covered, over a low heat for about 4 minutes. Be sure they don't burn. Let the mixture cool. Then beat into the yogurt. Stir in the lemon juice and coriander.
2. Shell and quarter the eggs, place in a shallow serving dish and cover with the spiced yogurt.

RICE SALAD

Preparation time: 10 minutes
Cooking time: 20 minutes

IMPERIAL (METRIC)	AMERICAN
10 oz (285g) patna rice	*1¼ cupsful patna rice*
1½ pints (900ml) vegetable stock	*3¾ cupsful vegetable stock*
½ lb (225g) French beans	*½ lb green beans*
1 red, 1 green and 1 yellow pepper	*1 red, 1 green and 1 yellow pepper*
1 fennel bulb	*1 fennel bulb*
Sea salt and freshly ground black pepper	*Sea salt and freshly ground black pepper*

1. Boil the rice in the vegetable stock until just tender; it should still be *al dente*. Allow to cool.
2. Trim the beans and cut into 1-inch (2.5cm) lengths. Cook in a little salted water until tender. Drain well and mix with the rice.
3. Thinly slice the peppers and fennel. Add to the rice mixture and combine thoroughly. Season to taste.

FRAISES À L'ORANGE (Strawberries with Orange)

Preparation time: 15 minutes
Marinating time: 2 hours

IMPERIAL (METRIC)
4 juicy oranges
4 tablespoonsful caster sugar
3 fl oz (90ml) orange curaçao
1 lb (450g) fresh strawberries

AMERICAN
4 juicy oranges
4 tablespoonsful superfine sugar
6 tablespoonsful orange curaçao
1 quart fresh strawberries

1. Grate the zest from two of the oranges and set aside. Peel all the oranges and remove all the pith. Slice the oranges thinly into a serving bowl (to catch all the juice) and remove the pips. Arrange the oranges attractively in the bottom of the bowl and sprinkle with half the sugar. Pour over the orange curaçao.
2. Hull the strawberries, halve the largest ones and arrange over the oranges. Mix the reserved orange zest with the rest of the sugar and sprinkle over the strawberries. Cover and leave to marinate in a cool place for 2 hours.
3. Before serving, turn the strawberries over carefully in the juice, not disturbing the oranges underneath.

SUMMER MENU 10

Asparagus with Parmesan Cheese	Frascati
Lettuce and Egg Gratin	Barolo
Artichokes and New Potatoes	
Mexican Beans	
Mixed Green Salad (See page 94)	
Cantal	
Delice de Saligny	
Iced Pineapple with Wild Strawberries	Sweet Champagne

ASPARAGUS WITH PARMESAN CHEESE

Cooking time: 15 minutes
Preparation time: 5 minutes
Baking time: 5 minutes

IMPERIAL (METRIC)
3 lb (1.3kg) asparagus spears
2 oz (55g) butter
Juice of 1 lemon
*Sea salt and freshly ground black
  pepper*
2 oz (55g) grated parmesan cheese

AMERICAN
3 lb asparagus spears
4 tablespoonsful butter
Juice of 1 lemon
*Sea salt and freshly ground black
  pepper*
½ cupful grated parmesan cheese

1. Boil the asparagus until tender. Drain carefully.
2. Preheat the oven to 400°F/200°C (Gas Mark 6).
3. Arrange the asparagus in a shallow earthenware dish. Melt the butter and lemon juice together. Pour over the asparagus. Season to taste. Sprinkle with the parmesan cheese and place in the oven until the cheese has melted, about 5 minutes.

LETTUCE AND EGG GRATIN

Preparation time: 15 minutes
Cooking time: 10 minutes
Baking time: 10 minutes

IMPERIAL (METRIC)	AMERICAN
1 large cos lettuce	*1 large leaf lettuce*
1 oz (30g) butter	*2 tablespoonsful butter*

Bechamel Sauce:

1 oz (30g) butter	*2 tablespoonsful butter*
1 tablespoonful flour	*1 tablespoonful flour*
½ pint (300ml) milk	*1¼ cupsful milk*
Sea salt and white pepper	*Sea salt and white pepper*
¼ pint (150ml) single cream	*⅔ cupful light cream*
6-8 hard-boiled eggs	*6-8 hard-cooked eggs*
2-4 tablespoonsful breadcrumbs	*2-4 tablespoonsful bread crumbs*

1. Wash and drain the lettuce. Slice it into strips and cook in the butter in a covered pan over a low heat for about 10 minutes. Set aside.
2. Make the bechamel sauce. Heat the butter, mix in the flour and cook for a minute. Add the milk slowly to make a smooth sauce, season with salt and pepper and remove from the heat. Add the sauce to the lettuce and stir in the cream.
3. Preheat the oven to 375°F/190°C (Gas Mark 5).
4. Shell and quarter the eggs and arrange in a shallow gratin dish. Pour the lettuce sauce over. Sprinkle with the breadcrumbs and bake for 10 minutes.

ARTICHOKES AND NEW POTATOES

Preparation time: 5 minutes
Cooking time: 25 minutes

IMPERIAL (METRIC)	AMERICAN
2 lb (900g) new potatoes, scrubbed	*2 lb new potatoes, scrubbed*
14-oz (395g) tin artichoke hearts	*14-oz can artichoke hearts*
2 oz (55g) butter	*4 tablespoonsful butter*
Sea salt and freshly ground black pepper	*Sea salt and freshly ground black pepper*
3 tablespoonsful chopped mint	*3 tablespoonsful chopped mint*

1. Boil the potatoes in their skins until tender.
2. Meanwhile, drain the artichoke hearts. Cut in half and place in a shallow earthenware dish, dot with the butter and place in a warm oven.
3. When the potatoes are cooked, drain well, add to the artichoke hearts, season to taste and toss well in the melted butter. Sprinkle with the mint.

MEXICAN BEANS

Cooking time: Cooking the kidney beans, plus 10 minutes

IMPERIAL (METRIC)
3 tablespoonsful olive oil
3 cloves garlic, crushed
1 large onion, diced
½ teaspoonful each: ground cumin,
   coriander and chilli powder
1 lb (450g) red kidney beans,
   cooked
Sea salt and freshly ground black
   pepper

AMERICAN
3 tablespoonsful olive oil
3 cloves garlic, crushed
1 large onion, diced
½ teaspoonful each: ground cumin,
   coriander and chili powder
1 lb red kidney beans, cooked
Sea salt and freshly ground black
   pepper

1.   Heat the olive oil in a large saucepan, cook the garlic, onion and spices until the onion is soft. Add the kidney beans, stir well, season to taste and reheat.

ICED PINEAPPLE WITH WILD STRAWBERRIES

Preparation time: 20 minutes
Chilling time: 2-3 hours

IMPERIAL (METRIC)
1 large or 2 medium-sized
   pineapples
1 lb (450g) wild strawberries, hulled
2 tablespoonsful caster sugar
2 tablespoonsful kirsch

AMERICAN
1 large or 2 medium-sized
   pineapples
1 lb wild strawberries (about 3
   cupsful), hulled
2 tablespoonsful superfine sugar
2 tablespoonsful kirsch

1.   Cut the top off the pineapple and reserve. Trim the base so that the pineapple sits squarely upright. Scoop out all the pineapple flesh, cut away the hard central core and discard. Cut the pineapple into cubes.
2.   Place the pineapple flesh in a bowl, add the strawberries, sugar and kirsch and marinate in the refrigerator for 2-3 hours. Place the pineapple rind container in the refrigerator to chill also.
3.   Just before serving, pile all the fruit and juices into the pineapple and replace the top.

SUMMER MENU 11

Gnocchi di Patate con Dolcelatte

Verduzzo Del Piave

Eggs and Spinach
Salsify Fritters
Peas with Couscous

Rioja

Barac
Blue Shropshire
Cheddar

Wild Strawberry Tartlets

Sweet Champagne

GNOCCHI DI PATATE CON DOLCELATTE
(Potato Gnocchi with Cheese)

Preparation time: 20 minutes
Cooking time: 45 minutes

IMPERIAL (METRIC)
1½ lb (680g) unpeeled floury
  potatoes
4 oz (115g) plain flour
1 egg
Sea salt and freshly ground black
  pepper

AMERICAN
1½ lb unpeeled floury potatoes
1 cupful all-purpose flour
1 egg
Sea salt and freshly ground black
  pepper

Sauce:
4 oz (115g) dolcelatte cheese
4 oz (115g) butter
Freshly ground black pepper

¼ lb dolcelatte cheese
½ cupful (1 stick) butter
Freshly ground black pepper

1. Boil the potatoes, then peel and purée. Add the flour and egg to the purée and mix until smooth. Season with salt and pepper. Mould into small balls about 1-inch (2.5cm) in diameter, then bend them into crescents and press the inside with the prongs of a fork.
2. Bring plenty of water to the boil in a large saucepan and add the gnocchi. They are done when they float to the surface. Remove with a slotted spoon and keep warm.
3. Make the sauce. Put the cheese, butter and pepper in a bowl over hot water and whisk until melted and thickened.
4. Pour the sauce over the gnocchi and place under a hot grill for a minute or two. Serve at once.

EGGS AND SPINACH

Preparation time: 10 minutes
Cooking time: 15 minutes
Baking time: 6-8 minutes

IMPERIAL (METRIC)	AMERICAN
1 lb (450g) leaf spinach	*1 lb leaf spinach*
6-8 eggs	*6-8 eggs*
½ pint (300ml) single cream	*1¼ cupsful light cream*
4 oz (115g) grated gruyère and parmesan cheese, mixed	*1 cupful grated unprocessed gruyère and parmesan cheese, mixed*
Sea salt and freshly ground black pepper	*Sea salt and freshly ground black pepper*

1. Wash the spinach, tear the leaves from the stalks into small scraps and discard the stalks. Cook the spinach in a covered saucepan with a little salt, but without water or butter over a low heat so that it doesn't burn. The spinach should be cooked within 10 minutes. Drain any liquid off, or raise the heat, uncover the pan and dry out. Turn into a shallow ovenproof dish.
2. Preheat the oven to 400°F/200°C (Gas Mark 6).
3. Make *oeufs mollets*, ie, plunge the eggs into a pan of boiling water and boil for 3-4 minutes, then plunge into the cold water. (The whites should be set and the yolks should be runny). Shell the eggs. Make hollows in the spinach and lay the eggs in. Pour the cream over and season to taste. Sprinkle with the cheese and bake for 6-8 minutes, or until the top starts to brown.

SALSIFY FRITTERS

Preparation time: 5 minutes
Cooking time: 15 minutes

IMPERIAL (METRIC)	AMERICAN
1 14-oz (395g) tin salsify	*1 14-oz can salsify (oyster plant)*
4 tablespoonsful double cream	*4 tablespoonsful heavy cream*
2 tablespoonsful flour	*2 tablespoonsful flour*
½ teaspoonful baking powder	*½ teaspoonful baking powder*
Sea salt and freshly ground black pepper	*Sea salt and freshly ground black pepper*
Corn oil for frying	*Corn oil for frying*

1. Drain the salsify. Mash into a rough purée with a fork. Add the rest of the ingredients, except the oil and mix well.
2. Heat a little corn oil in a frying pan and drop spoonsful of the mixture in; flatten into small cakes. Fry on both sides until golden brown. After they are done, keep warm in the oven.

PEAS WITH COUSCOUS

Standing time: 10 minutes
Cooking time: 45 minutes

IMPERIAL (METRIC)	AMERICAN
½ lb (225g) couscous	*1 cupful couscous*
½ pint (300ml) cold water	*1¼ cupsfuls cold water*
1 pint (600ml) vegetable stock	*2½ cupsful vegetable stock*
1 lb (450g) shelled peas	*1 lb shelled peas*
4 oz (115g) butter	*½ cupful (1 stick) butter*
Sea salt and freshly ground black pepper	*Sea salt and freshly ground black pepper*

1. Place couscous in a bowl and pour over the cold water. Leave for 10 minutes to absorb, then transfer the couscous to a steamer and steam over the vegetable stock for 40 minutes.
2. Cook the peas in boiling salted water until tender, then drain.
3. Mix couscous, peas and butter together and season to taste.

WILD STRAWBERRY TARTLETS

Preparation time: Making the pastry, plus 20 minutes
Standing time: 1-2 hours
Baking time: 10 minutes

IMPERIAL (METRIC)	AMERICAN
1 bunch mint, finely chopped	*1 bunch mint, finely chopped*
1 pint (600ml) crème fraîche or 1¼ lb (565g) Quark	*2½ cupsful crème fraîche or 1¼ lb low-fat cheese*
Sweet pastry (see Tarte au Citron, page 64)	*Sweet pastry (see Tarte au Citron, page 64)*
1 lb (450g) wild strawberries	*1 lb (about 3 cupsful) wild strawberries*
Icing sugar	*Confectioner's sugar*

1. Stir the mint into the crème fraîche and leave to macerate for 1-2 hours.
2. Prepare the pastry and refrigerate for 1 hour.
3. Preheat the oven to 375°F/190°C (Gas Mark 5).
4. Roll out the pastry very thinly and line 6-8 tartlet cases (3-inch/7.5cm). Bake until golden, about 10 minutes. Allow to cool.
5. Hull the strawberries. Fill the tartlets with the crème fraîche and arrange the strawberries on top. A few minutes before serving, dust with the icing sugar.

Note: To prepare crème fraîche, place ½ pint/300ml/1¼ cupsful double cream in a screw top jar, mix in 1 teaspoonful buttermilk and store in a warm place, away from draughts for 24-36 hours. Then refrigerate. It will keep for 2-3 weeks.

SUMMER MENU 12

Iced Borscht   Frascati

Gnocchi alla Genovese   Barbera d'Asti
Pepperonata
Fèves à la Poulette

Pecorino Pepato
Windsor Red
Reblochon

Apricot Cream Cheese   Monbazillac

ICED BORSCHT (Iced Beetroot Soup)

Preparation time: 15 minutes
Cooking time: 2-3 hours
Chilling time: 2 hours-1 day

IMPERIAL (METRIC)	AMERICAN
1 lb (450g) raw beetroot	*1 lb raw beets*
2 onions, diced	*2 onions, diced*
2 cloves garlic, crushed	*2 cloves garlic, crushed*
2 celery hearts, sliced	*2 celery hearts, sliced*
3 pints (1.8 litres) boiling water	*7½ cupsful boiling water*
Juice of 1 lemon	*Juice of 1 lemon*
Sea salt and freshly ground black pepper	*Sea salt and freshly ground black pepper*
Soured cream to serve	*Sour cream to serve*

1. Reserve 1 beetroot. Peel and dice the remainder and add with the onions, garlic and celery to the boiling water. Simmer for 2-3 hours, topping up with more water if necessary. Cool.

2. Purée all the vegetables in a blender and put through a sieve. Add the lemon juice and seasoning to the stock. Chill in the refrigerator. Grate the remaining beetroot and leave in ½ pint/300ml/1¼ cupsful water for several hours, then add this stock to the rest of the soup to improve the colour.

3. Serve with ice cubes floating on the surface and pass around a large bowl of soured cream for guests to help themselves.

GNOCCHI ALLA GENOVESE

Cooking time: 25 minutes (before and after chilling)
Chilling time: Several hours

IMPERIAL (METRIC)	AMERICAN
1 pint (600ml) milk	*2½ cupsful milk*
Sea salt and freshly ground black pepper	*Sea salt and freshly ground black pepper*
Pinch of nutmeg	*Pinch of nutmeg*
6 oz (170g) fine semolina	*1½ cupsful fine semolina*
2 oz (55g) grated parmesan cheese	*½ cupful grated parmesan cheese*
2 eggs, beaten	*2 eggs, beaten*

1. Bring milk to the boil with the salt, pepper and nutmeg. Pour in the semolina stir until it becomes a thick mass. Remove from the heat.
2. Add the cheese and beaten eggs to the semolina and stir until it is smooth and comes away from the sides of the pan. Spread it onto a flat dish in a ½-inch (1.25cm) thick layer. Chill for several hours.
3. Cut the chilled semolina into small squares and with floured hands, form into cork shapes. Lay on a floured board.
4. Have a large pan of boiling salted water ready. Throw in the gnocchi and simmer for 3-4 minutes (they will rise to the surface when done). Remove with a slotted spoon and keep warm. Serve with hot butter and garlic sauce, pesto (either commercial sauce from Italian shops, or homemade) or tomato sauce (see page 84).

PESTO

Preparation time: 5 minutes

IMPERIAL (METRIC)	AMERICAN
6 tablespoonsful chopped fresh basil	*6 tablespoonsful chopped fresh basil*
2 oz (55g) pine nuts	*½ cupful pine nuts*
2 oz (55g) grated parmesan cheese	*½ cupful grated parmesan cheese*
Juice of 1 lemon	*Juice of 1 lemon*
2 cloves garlic, crushed	*2 cloves garlic, crushed*
¼ pint (150ml) olive oil	*⅔ cupful olive oil*

1. Mix all the ingredients together in a blender. You may need a little more olive oil. The sauce should be thick, but not too stiff. Commercial pesto can be thinned out with olive oil. If you grow your own basil in the summer (it is an annual and needs to be grown under glass in England), there is no greater sauce. It gives the highest satisfaction to the palate and is a sublime treat.

Note: To preserve fresh basil for use in other seasons, harvest the leaves and blend with lemon juice, garlic and olive oil, then freeze. To use, bring up to room temperature, then blend in the pine nuts and parmesan cheese.

PEPERONATA

Preparation time: 10 minutes
Cooking time: 35 minutes

IMPERIAL (METRIC)	AMERICAN
6 large red peppers	*6 large red peppers*
6 large tomatoes	*6 large tomatoes*
1 large onion	*1 large onion*
1 oz (30g) butter	*2 tablespoonsful butter*
2 tablespoonsful olive oil	*2 tablespoonsful olive oil*
3 cloves garlic, crushed	*3 cloves garlic, crushed*
Sea salt and freshly ground black pepper	*Sea salt and freshly ground black pepper*

1. Deseed peppers and cut into strips. Peel and chop tomatoes. Slice the onion thinly. Heat the butter and oil in a saucepan and cook the peppers, onions and garlic, covered, for about 15 minutes or until they are soft.
2. Add the tomatoes and seasoning. Continue to cook for another 20 minutes over a low heat, so that most of the oil is absorbed.

FÈVES À LA POULETTE (Broad Beans in Parsley Sauce)

Preparation time: 5 minutes
Cooking time: 15 minutes

IMPERIAL (METRIC)	AMERICAN
2 lb (900g) broad beans, shelled	*2 lb fava beans, shelled*
1 oz (30g) butter	*2 tablespoonsful butter*
1 teaspoonful flour	*1 teaspoonful flour*
2 egg yolks, beaten	*2 egg yolks, beaten*
Handful of chopped parsley	*Handful of chopped parsley*

1. Cook the beans in boiling salted water until tender. Reserve about ¼ pint/150ml/⅔ cupful of the cooking water and discard the rest.
2. Melt the butter, stir in the flour and add the reserved water to make a light sauce. Add the beans and let them cook in the sauce for a few minutes, then stir in the egg yolks and let the sauce thicken. Sprinkle with chopped parsley and serve.

APRICOT CREAM CHEESE

Preparation time: 15 minutes

IMPERIAL (METRIC)	AMERICAN
8 fresh apricots	*8 fresh apricots*
2 oz (55g) caster sugar	*¼ cupful superfine sugar*
12 fl oz (360ml) crème fraîche or	*1½ cupsful crème fraîche or ¾ lb*
¾ lb (340g) Quark	*low-fat cheese*
2 tablespoonsful apricot brandy	*2 tablespoonsful apricot brandy*
2 glacé apricots, chopped	*2 glacé apricots, chopped*

1. Peel the apricots by briefly plunging into boiling water. Cut in half, stone and arrange in a serving dish. Sprinkle with a little of the sugar.
2. Mix all the remaining ingredients together and heap over the apricots.

SUMMER MENU 13

Gâteaux d'Asperges	Chardonnay
Pain d'Épinards	Chambertin
Confit Bayeldi	
Purée aux Pommes de Terre	
Mixed Green Salad (See page 94)	
Chamois d'Or	
Gorgonzola con Mascarpone	
Mature Cheddar	
Iced Stuffed Melons	Monbazillac

GÂTEAUX D'ASPERGES (Asparagus Gâteaux)

Preparation time: 10 minutes
Baking time: 20 minutes

IMPERIAL (METRIC)
2 14-oz (395g) tins asparagus spears
4 eggs
½ pint (300ml) single cream
Sea salt and freshly ground black pepper
Pinch of nutmeg
2 oz (55g) grated gruyère cheese
1-2 tablespoonsful butter
Tomato sauce to serve (see page 84)

AMERICAN
2 14-oz cans asparagus spears
4 eggs
1¼ cupsful light cream
Sea salt and freshly ground black pepper
Pinch of nutmeg
½ cupful grated unprocessed gruyère cheese
1-2 tablespoonsful butter
Tomato sauce to serve (see page 84)

1. Drain the asparagus spears. Cut the tips off each spear and reserve for garnish.
2. Preheat the oven to 425°F/220°C (Gas Mark 7).
3. Place the remainder of the asparagus in a blender container. Add the eggs, cream, seasoning and nutmeg. Blend to a thin purée. Add the grated cheese.
4. Butter 6-8 china ramekins and divide the asparagus purée among them. Place the ramekins in a baking tin and pour boiling water halfway up the sides. Bake for 20 minutes or until a knife, inserted into the centre comes out clean.
5. Turn out on individual plates. Decorate the tops with reserved asparagus tips and pour a little tomato sauce around the base of each gâteau.

PAIN D'ÉPINARDS (Spinach Mould)

Preparation time: 15 minutes
Cooking time: 12 minutes
Baking time: 45-55 minutes

IMPERIAL (METRIC)
1½ lb (680g) leaf spinach
1½ oz (40g) butter
¾ pint (450ml) milk
3 eggs, beaten
Sea salt and freshly ground black
  pepper
1½ oz (40g) fresh breadcrumbs
Watercress to garnish

AMERICAN
1½ lb leaf spinach
3 tablespoonsful butter
2 cupsful milk
3 eggs, beaten
Sea salt and freshly ground black
  pepper
¾ cupful fresh bread crumbs
Watercress to garnish

1. Remove the stalks from the spinach. Take 6-8 of the largest leaves and blanch them in boiling water for 2 minutes. Slice the rest of the spinach and cook it in half the butter in a covered saucepan for about 10 minutes.
2. Butter a 1¾ pint/1 litre/1 quart charlotte mould with the rest of the butter. Line the mould with the blanched spinach, leaving enough overlap so that the spinach can be folded over to cover the top of the mould.
3. Preheat the oven to 350°F/180°C (Gas Mark 4).
4. Add the milk, eggs, seasoning and breadcrumbs to the rest of the spinach and mix well. Pour into the charlotte mould and cover the top with the overlapping spinach leaves. Place the mould in a baking dish, pour boiling water halfway up the sides of the mould and bake for 45-55 minutes.
5. Life the mould from its water bath and let it cool a little, about 5 minutes. Unmould onto a platter and garnish with watercress.

CONFIT BAYELDI

Preparation time: 10 minutes
Baking time: 30 minutes

IMPERIAL (METRIC)	AMERICAN
2-3 courgettes	*2-3 zucchini*
2 small aubergines	*2 small eggplants*
½ lb (225g) button mushrooms	*½ lb button mushrooms*
6 large tomatoes	*6 large tomatoes*
½ teaspoonful thyme	*½ teaspoonful thyme*
½ teaspoonful sage	*½ teaspoonful sage*
2 tablespoonsful olive oil	*2 tablespoonsful olive oil*
Sea salt and freshly ground black pepper	*Sea salt and freshly ground black pepper*

1. Preheat the oven to 400°F/200°C (Gas Mark 6). Pare courgettes and aubergines (eggplants) in stripes, lengthways (merely for decorative purposes), then slice. Cut the mushrooms in half lengthways. Slice the unpeeled tomatoes.
2. In a large, shallow earthenware dish, arrange the vegetables in rows overlapping each other. Start with the courgettes, then add the tomatoes, mushrooms and aubergines, continuing until all the ingredients are used. Sprinkle with the herbs, olive oil and seasoning and bake for 30 minutes.

PURÉE AUX POMMES DE TERRE (Potato Purée)

Preparation time: 5 minutes
Cooking time: 25 minutes

IMPERIAL (METRIC)	AMERICAN
2 lb (900g) potatoes	*2 lb potatoes*
2 tablespoonsful milk	*2 tablespoonsful milk*
3 tablespoonsful double cream	*3 tablespoonsful heavy cream*
2 oz (55g) butter	*4 tablespoonsful butter*
Sea salt and freshly ground black pepper	*Sea salt and freshly ground black pepper*

1. Boil potatoes until tender. Drain well. Put back on the heat to dry out any moisture. Mash the potatoes.
2. Add all the other ingredients and mix well, beating with a whisk to eliminate any lumps. Spoon into a shallow ovenproof dish and keep warm.

ICED STUFFED MELON

Preparation time: 15 minutes
Chilling time: 4 hours

IMPERIAL (METRIC)	AMERICAN
3-4 very small Ogen melons	*3-4 very small cantaloupes*
1 orange	*1 orange*
1 grapefruit	*1 grapefruit*
4 kiwi fruit	*4 kiwi fruit*
1 lb (450g) mixture of strawberries, raspberries or other summer berries	*About 3 cupsful mixture of strawberries, raspberries or other summer berries*
2 tablespoonsful caster sugar	*2 tablespoonsful superfine sugar*
4 tablespoonsful framboise liqueur	*4 tablespoonsful framboise liqueur*
Mint leaves to garnish	*Mint leaves to garnish*

1. Cut melons in half and scoop out the seeds and pith. Keeping the shells intact, cut out the flesh and slice into a large bowl.
2. Remove the skin, pith and pips from the orange and grapefruit, slice the fruit and add to the melon. Peel and slice the kiwi fruit and add to the other fruit with the sugar and framboise.
3. Mix gently, but well and chill the fruit and melon shells for 4 hours. To serve, fill the shells with the fruit and decorate with mint leaves.

AUTUMN MENUS

AUTUMN MENU 1

Pumpkin Soup   **Barsac**

Stuffed Marrow   **Beaune de Château**
Glazed Turnips
Baked Potatoes with Capers

Double Gloucester
Camembert

Quince Syllabub   **Armagnac**

PUMPKIN SOUP

Preparation time: 10 minutes
Cooking time: 25 minutes, plus reheating

IMPERIAL (METRIC)	AMERICAN
2 lb (900g) pumpkin flesh	*2 lb pumpkin flesh*
3 oz (85g) butter	*6 tablespoonsful butter*
Sea salt and freshly ground black	*Sea salt and freshly ground black*
pepper	*pepper*
2½ pints (1.5 litres) vegetable stock	*6 cupsful vegetable stock*

1. Remove rind and deseed the pumpkin. Dice the flesh and sauté in the butter. Add salt and pepper to taste and cook for another 2-3 minutes.
2. Add vegetable stock, bring to the boil and simmer for 20 minutes. Leave to cool, then blend to a thin purée.
3. Reheat before serving.

STUFFED MARROW

Preparation time: 15 minutes
Cooking time: 10 minutes
Baking time: 1 hour

IMPERIAL (METRIC)	AMERICAN
1 2½-3 lb (1.25kg) marrow	*1 2½-3 lb marrow or butternut*
1 lb (450g) mushrooms	* squash*
2 oz (55g) butter	*1 lb mushrooms*
2 onions, diced	*4 tablespoonsful butter*
5 cloves garlic, crushed	*2 onions, diced*
1 teaspoonful chopped sage	*5 cloves garlic, crushed*
1 teaspoonful chopped thyme	*1 teaspoonful chopped sage*
1 teaspoonful chopped chervil	*1 teaspoonful chopped thyme*
4 oz (115g) curd cheese	*1 teaspoonful chopped chervil*
2 eggs	*½ cupful curd cheese*
Sea salt and freshly ground black	*2 eggs*
* pepper*	*Sea salt and freshly ground black*
Watercress to garnish	* pepper*
	Watercress to garnish

1. Cut a lid from the marrow (squash) along its length. Scoop out the seeds and discard and set the lid aside. Remove all the seeds and pith from the marrow cavity.
2. Slice the mushrooms thinly, melt the butter in a pan and cook the mushrooms, onion, garlic and herbs until they are soft, about 10 minutes. Cool.
3. Place the cooked vegetables in a blender container and purée. Add the cheese, eggs and seasoning. Pour into the marrow cavity and replace the lid.
4. Preheat the oven to 450°F/230°C (Gas Mark 8).
5. Wrap the marrow tightly in foil. Place on a baking sheet and bake for 1 hour. Remove from the oven and allow to rest for about 10 minutes before unwrapping the foil. Serve surrounded by glazed turnips on a platter. Decorate with watercress.

GLAZED TURNIPS

Preparation time: 5 minutes
Cooking time: 10 minutes

IMPERIAL (METRIC)	AMERICAN
2 lb (900g) young turnips	*2 lb young turnips*
2 oz (55g) butter	*4 tablespoonsful butter*
2 tablespoonsful raw cane sugar	*2 tablespoonsful raw cane sugar*
Sea salt and freshly ground black	*Sea salt and freshly ground black*
* pepper*	* pepper*

1. Halve or quarter the turnips and cook in a little boiling salted water for 5 minutes. Drain well.
2. Melt the butter in a pan and sauté the turnips, adding the sugar, salt and pepper and turning them over until the sugar has caramelized.

BAKED POTATOES WITH CAPERS

Preparation time: 5 minutes
Baking time: 1¼ hours

IMPERIAL (METRIC)	AMERICAN
6-8 baking potatoes	*6-8 baking potatoes*
4 oz (115g) capers	*1 cupful capers*
½ pint (300ml) soured cream	*1¼ cupsful sour cream*
Sea salt and freshly ground black	*Sea salt and freshly ground black*
* pepper*	* pepper*

1.   Preheat the oven to 350°F/180°C (Gas Mark 4).
2.   Bake the potatoes for 1 hour. When they are done, remove from the oven and split in half, lengthways. Scoop out the potato from each skin and place in a large bowl. Reserve the skins.
3.   Add the capers, soured cream and seasoning to the baked potato and mash well.
4.   Fill the potato skins with the mixture and replace in a hot oven for 10-15 minutes, or until the tops of the potatoes begin to brown and crisp.

QUINCE SYLLABUB

Preparation time: 10 minutes
Cooking time: 20 minutes
Chilling time: 2 hours

IMPERIAL (METRIC)	AMERICAN
2 large quinces	*2 large quinces*
2 tablespoonsful water	*2 tablespoonsful water*
2 eggs, separated	*2 eggs, separated*
2 tablespoonsful honey	*2 tablespoonsful honey*
1 pint (600ml) double cream	*2½ cupsful heavy cream*

1.   Peel and core the quinces. Dice the flesh and cook in the measured water for about 20 minutes. Let cool.
2.   Put the quinces and water into a blender container with the egg yolks and honey. Blend to a smooth purée.
3.   Whisk the egg whites until stiff. Whip the cream until stiff. Fold both into the purée, pile into a glass serving dish and chill for about 2 hours.

AUTUMN MENU 2

Glamorgan Sausages	**Torricella**
Courge au Beurre Noir **Gâteau de Pommes de Terre** **Runner Beans** **Salade de Romaine aux Capucines**	**Rubesco di Torgiano**
Romano **Gorgonzola**	
Whim-Wham	**Eau de Vie**

Note: This meal begins and ends with English recipes, the wines and cheese are Italian and the main course and salad are French.

GLAMORGAN SAUSAGES

Preparation time: 20 minutes
Cooking time: Making tomato sauce, plus 12 minutes

IMPERIAL (METRIC)	AMERICAN
6 oz (170g) grated lancashire cheese	*1½ cupsful grated cheddar cheese*
4 oz (115g) fresh wholemeal breadcrumbs	*2 cupsful fresh wholewheat bread crumbs*
3 tablespoonsful chopped spring onions	*3 tablespoonsful chopped scallions*
3 egg yolks	*3 egg yolks*
2 tablespoonsful chopped parsley	*2 tablespoonsful chopped parsley*
½ teaspoonful chopped thyme	*½ teaspoonful chopped thyme*
1 teaspoonful mustard powder	*1 teaspoonful powdered mustard*
Sea salt and freshly ground black pepper	*Sea salt and freshly ground black pepper*
1 egg white	*1 egg white*
Wholemeal breadcrumbs for coating	*Wholewheat bread crumbs for coating*
Sunflower oil for frying	*Sunflower oil for frying*
Lettuce leaves to garnish	*Lettuce leaves to garnish*
Hot tomato sauce to serve (see page 84)	*Hot tomato sauce to serve (see page 84)*

1. Mix all the ingredients, up to and including the pepper, together in a bowl, or better still in a food processor. If the mixture is too dry to stick together, add another egg yolk.

2. Shape the mixture into 12-16 small sausages, dip each one in egg white and roll in breadcrumbs to cover.

3. Heat the oil in a frying pan and fry the 'sausages' until golden brown. (They may be kept warm in the oven for a while.)

4. Serve the 'sausages' on a bed of iceberg or cos lettuce, accompanied with hot tomato sauce.

COURGE AU BEURRE NOIR (Sautéed Pumpkin with Beurre Noir)

Preparation time: 5 minutes
Cooking time: 15 minutes

IMPERIAL (METRIC)
A little flour for dusting
Olive oil for frying
6-8 slices of pumpkin, 3 × 3 × ¼
  inches (7.5 × 7.5 × .5cm)
2-3 oz (55-85g) butter
Juice of 1 lemon
3 tablespoonsful capers
Sea salt and freshly ground black
  pepper

AMERICAN
A little flour for dusting
Olive oil for frying
6-8 slices of pumpkin, 3 × 3 × ¼
  inches
4-6 tablespoonsful butter
Juice of 1 lemon
3 tablespoonsful capers
Sea salt and freshly ground black
  pepper

1. Dust the pumpkin slices with a little flour.

2. Heat the oil in a frying pan and sauté the pumpkin until it is crisp and golden, about 4 minutes each side. Keep warm in the oven.

3. In another pan, heat the butter until it begins to brown, then add the lemon juice, capers and seasoning. Pour over the pumpkin and serve.

GÂTEAU DE POMMES DE TERRE (Potato Gâteau)

Preparation time: 20 minutes
Baking time: 50 minutes

IMPERIAL (METRIC)	AMERICAN
13-oz packet frozen puff pastry, defrosted	*¾ package (17¼ oz) frozen puff pastry, defrosted*
1½ lb (680g) new potatoes, scraped	*1½ lb new potatoes, scraped*
5 oz (140g) diced onion	*1 cupful diced onion*
4 cloves garlic, sliced	*4 cloves garlic, sliced*
2 oz (55g) butter	*4 tablespoonsful butter*
Sea salt and freshly ground black pepper	*Sea salt and freshly ground black pepper*
Grated nutmeg	*Grated nutmeg*
8 fl oz (240ml) single cream	*1 cupful light cream*
1 egg, beaten	*1 egg, beaten*
1 tablespoonful each: chopped parsley, chervil, chives, dill	*1 tablespoonful each: chopped parsley, chervil, chives, dill*

1. Roll out the pastry and use half to line a 10-inch (25cm) flan dish or shallow cake tin.
2. Preheat the oven to 450°F/230°C (Gas Mark 8).
3. Slice the potatoes thinly either on a mandoline or in a food processor. Blanch for 2 minutes in boiling salted water. Drain and pat dry.
4. Arrange the potato slices on the pastry, interleaving with the onion and garlic. Dot each layer with butter and season with salt, pepper and nutmeg. Pour in half the cream and cover with the remaining pastry.
5. Make a hole in the centre of the pastry. Decorate the pie with pastry leaves, made from the trimmings. Mix the egg with the remaining cream and brush the top of the pastry with a little of the mixture.
6. Protect the top of the pastry with a piece of buttered greaseproof paper and bake for 30-40 minutes. Remove from the oven.
7. Stir the herbs into the remaining egg and cream mixture. Pour through the hole in the pastry, remove the greaseproof paper and replace the gâteau in the oven for a further 5-10 minutes, until the top is nicely browned.

RUNNER BEANS

Preparation time: 10 minutes
Cooking time: 3-4 minutes

I think runner beans are superb, with a distinct and delicious flavour (why the French do not grow or eat them is a mystery). They should be picked young, not more than 5 inches (12.5cm) long, sliced diagonally if you wish, but this was a method devised for old, tough beans; young ones can be sliced in chunks after being topped and tailed. Either boil them in a little salted water for 3-4 minutes or steam them for slightly longer. They must not be overcooked, for then they are soft and soggy. So watch them — they should still be a little resistant to the bite — *al dente*. Cook them between courses. Your guests can wait. Simple vegetables soon deteriorate if left hanging around to keep warm.

SALADE DE ROMAINE AUX CAPUCINES (Lettuce and Nasturtium Salad)

Preparation time: 10 minutes

IMPERIAL (METRIC)
For the dressing:
Juice of 1 lemon
3 tablespoonsful olive oil
Sea salt and freshly ground black
  pepper

1 large cos or iceberg lettuce
20-30 nasturtium leaves
10-12 nasturtium flowers

AMERICAN

Juice of 1 lemon
3 tablespoonsful olive oil
Sea salt and freshly ground black
  pepper

1 large leaf or iceberg lettuce
20-30 nasturtium leaves
10-12 nasturtium flowers

1.   First make the dressing by mixing the lemon juice, olive oil and seasoning together in a large salad bowl.
2.   Tear the lettuce into manageable pieces and arrange in the bowl.
3.   Cut the nasturtium leaves into strips and sprinkle over the lettuce. Arrange the flowers in all their brilliant colours over the top.
4.   The salad can be tossed just before it is eaten; the flowers are edible.

WHIM-WHAM

Preparation time: 15 minutes

IMPERIAL (METRIC)
3-4 ripe pears
6-8 boudoir biscuits
2 tablespoonsful sweet sherry
4 tablespoonsful double cream
1 tablespoonful chopped roasted
  hazelnuts
Candied orange peel to decorate

AMERICAN
3-4 ripe pears
6-8 ladyfingers
2 tablespoonsful sweet sherry
4 tablespoonsful heavy cream
1 tablespoonful chopped roasted
  hazelnuts (filberts)
Candied orange peel to decorate

1.   Allow one pear half per person. Pare, halve and core the pears and place in a large dish. Place 1 biscuit on top of each pear and sprinkle a little sherry on top of each biscuit.
2.   Whip the cream until stiff. Place a dollop of cream on each portion, sprinkle with the nuts and decorate with candied orange peel.

Note: Whim-Wham means something trifling.

AUTUMN MENU 3
(Illustrated between pages 168 and 169.)

Two-Pear Salad	Graves or Sauvignon
Tomato and Oatmeal Tart	Gevrey-Chambertin or
Sage and Apple Potatoes	Saint-Emilion
Watercress and Endive Salad	
Delice de Saint Cyr	
Reblochon	
Camembert	
Blackberry Fool	Armagnac or Calvados

TWO-PEAR SALAD

Preparation time: 20 minutes

IMPERIAL (METRIC)
1 crisp lettuce heart
*2 large, ripe avocados, peeled and
  stoned*
*2 large, ripe conference pears, pared
  and cored*
1 tablespoonful tarragon vinegar
2 teaspoonful tarragon mustard
¼ pint (150ml) soured cream
Handful of chopped tarragon

AMERICAN
1 crisp lettuce heart
*2 large, ripe avocados, peeled and
  stoned*
*2 large, ripe bartlett pears, pared
  and cored*
1 tablespoonful tarragon vinegar
2 teaspoonful tarragon mustard
⅔ cupful sour cream
Handful of chopped tarragon

1. Arrange lettuce leaves on 6-8 individual plates. Cut the avocados and conference pears into thin slices. Arrange on the plates, interleaving both types of pears.
2. Mix the vinegar and mustard and stir into the soured cream. Spoon over the pears. Sprinkle with the chopped tarragon.

TOMATO AND OATMEAL TART

Preparation time: 20 minutes
Chilling time: 1 hour
Cooking time: 20 minutes
Baking time: 30 minutes

IMPERIAL (METRIC)

Pastry:
4 oz (115g) plain flour
4 oz (115g) rolled oats
1 teaspoonful sea salt
4 oz (115g) butter or margarine
1 large egg, beaten

For the Filling:
1 lb (450g) tomatoes
2 dried red chillies
¼ pint (150ml) red wine
2 oz (55g) butter
1 large onion, diced
3 cloves garlic, crushed
2 oz (55g) grated cheddar cheese
2 oz (55g) grated parmesan cheese
1 large egg
3 tablespoonsful single cream
Sea salt and freshly ground black
 pepper

AMERICAN

1 cupful all-purpose flour
1 cupful rolled oats
1 teaspoonful sea salt
½ cupful (1 stick) butter or
 margarine
1 large egg, beaten

1 lb tomatoes
2 dried red chili peppers
⅔ cupful red wine
4 tablespoonsful butter
1 large onion, diced
3 cloves garlic, crushed
½ cupful grated cheddar cheese
½ cupful grated parmesan cheese
1 large egg
3 tablespoonsful light cream
Sea salt and freshly ground black
 pepper

1. Make the pastry in the usual manner. Line a 8-9-inch (20-22.5cm) tart tin with a removable base. Let it rest for an hour or so in the refrigerator.
2. Cook the tomatoes, chillies and red wine together in a covered saucepan for about 10 minutes. Leave to cool. Remove chillies and discard. Sieve the tomato mixture, then reduce the sauce by about one-half over a high heat.
3. Preheat the oven to 375°F/190°C (Gas Mark 5).
4. Add the cheeses, egg and cream to the reduced tomato sauce. Mix well. Season with salt and pepper and pour into the pastry case. Place on a warmed baking sheet and bake for 30 minutes.

Note: The top of the tart may be sprinkled with additional grated cheddar cheese and breadcrumbs. Or make a lattice or pastry flowers with leftover pastry. Or sprinkle with cheese and breadcrumbs and decorate the centre with pastry flowers. It is at its best if served warm.

SAGE AND APPLE POTATOES

Preparation time: Baking the potatoes, plus 10 minutes
Baking time: 20 minutes

IMPERIAL (METRIC)	AMERICAN
6-8 baked potatoes	*6-8 baked potatoes*
2 handfuls chopped sage leaves	*2 handfuls chopped sage leaves*
4 oz (115g) butter	*½ cupful (1 stick) butter*
Sea salt and freshly ground black pepper	*Sea salt and freshly ground black pepper*
1 lb (450g) cooking apples, sliced	*1 lb cooking apples, sliced*

1. Cut the baked potatoes in half lengthways and scoop out the flesh. Reserve the shells and place the potato in a large mixing bowl with the sage and half of the butter. Season with salt and pepper and mix well.
2. Pile the mixture into the potato shells. Cover with apple slices and dot with the remaining butter. (All this can be done in advance.)
3. Preheat the oven to 400°F/200°C (Gas Mark 6).
4. Bake the potatoes for about 20 minutes, or until the potato puffs up and the apple melts.

WATERCRESS AND ENDIVE SALAD

Preparation time: 10 minutes

IMPERIAL (METRIC)	AMERICAN
2 bunches watercress	*2 bunches watercress*
4 endives	*4 heads chicory*
Sea salt and freshly ground black pepper	*Sea salt and freshly ground black pepper*
1 teaspoonful lemon juice	*1 teaspoonful lemon juice*
2 tablespoonsful walnut oil	*2 tablespoonsful walnut oil*

1. Cut the stalks off the watercress and discard. Separate the endives (chicory) into leaves.
2. Mix seasoning, lemon juice and walnut oil together.
3. Pile the watercress in the centre of a large platter, then arrange the endive (chicory) around it, pointing outwards. Dribble a little dressing over each leaf.

162

BLACKBERRY FOOL

Preparation time: 10 minutes
Cooking time: 15 minutes

IMPERIAL (METRIC)
2 lb (900g) blackberries
3 fl oz (90ml) sweet sherry
2 tablespoonsful honey
1 pint (600ml) double cream
Boudoir biscuits to serve
Crystallized violets (optional) to
    decorate

AMERICAN
2 lb blackberries (about 1½ quarts)
6 tablespoonsful sweet sherry
2 tablespoonsful honey
2½ cupsful heavy cream
Ladyfingers to serve
Crystallized violets (optional) to
    decorate

1. Cook the blackberries in the sherry until soft. Pour off most of the liquid and reserve.
    Purée the fruit in a blender, sieve and set aside.
2. Pour the reserved liquid into a saucepan, add the honey and reduce over a high heat
    until about one-half or one-third the quantity is left. Leave to cool, then add to the
    fruit purée.
3. Whip the cream until stiff and fold it into the fruit. Pile into individual glasses and
    serve with a boudoir biscuit. If so minded, decorate with crystallized violets. This dessert
    looks stunning.

AUTUMN MENU 4

Brussels Sprouts Purée	Fendant
Stuffed Mushrooms Kartoffelpuffer Creamed Chicory	Rioja Reserva
Farmhouse Mature Cheddar Pont l'Evêque	
Damson Cream	Eau de Vie or Calvados

BRUSSELS SPROUTS PURÉE

Preparation time: 15 minutes
Cooking time: 6 minutes

IMPERIAL (METRIC)
1 lb (450g) Brussels sprouts,
*   trimmed (fresh or frozen)*
6 oz (170g) white bread, crusts
*   removed*
2 tablespoonsful lemon juice
5 tablespoonsful sunflower oil
¼ whole nutmeg, grated
Sea salt
½ teaspoonful cayenne pepper
1 teaspoonful paprika
½ tablespoonful olive oil
Wholemeal toast or pitta bread to
*   serve*

AMERICAN
1 lb Brussels sprouts, trimmed (fresh
*   or frozen)*
6 slices white bread, crusts removed
2 tablespoonsful lemon juice
5 tablespoonsful sunflower oil
¼ whole nutmeg, grated
Sea salt
½ teaspoonful cayenne pepper
1 teaspoonful paprika
½ tablespoonful olive oil
Wholewheat toast or pita bread to
*   serve*

1. Boil the sprouts until tender. Drain.
2. Dip the bread into water, then squeeze dry.
3. Place the sprouts, bread, lemon juice and sunflower oil into a blender container and blend until smooth. Season with nutmeg, salt and cayenne pepper.
3. Refrigerate or keep cool.
4. Turn into a serving dish. Mix the paprika and olive oil and dribble in a pattern over the surface. Serve with wholemeal toast or pitta bread.

STUFFED MUSHROOMS

Preparation time: 10 minutes
Cooking time: 5 minutes
Baking time: 30 minutes

IMPERIAL (METRIC)	AMERICAN
6-8 large, unbroken mushrooms	*6-8 large, unbroken mushrooms*
1 large onion, diced	*1 large onion, diced*
2 oz (55g) butter	*4 tablespoonsful butter*
3 cloves garlic, crushed	*3 cloves garlic, crushed*
1 tablespoonful chopped sage	*1 tablespoonful chopped sage*
1 tablespoonful chopped dillweed	*1 tablespoonful chopped dillweed*
1 tablespoonful chopped marjoram	*1 tablespoonful chopped marjoram*
4 oz (115g) wholemeal breadcrumbs	*2 cupsful wholewheat breadcrumbs*
3 tablespoonsful grated gruyère cheese	*3 tablespoonsful grated unprocessed gruyère cheese*
Sea salt and freshly ground black pepper to taste	*Sea salt and freshly ground black pepper to taste*

1. Carefully separate the mushroom caps from the stems and set the caps aside. Chop the stems, add to the onion and sauté both in the butter until soft. Stir in the garlic and herbs.
2. Preheat the oven to 350°F/180°C (Gas Mark 4).
3. Place the breadcrumbs and cheese in a mixing bowl. Add the onion and mushroom mixture, stir well and season to taste.
4. Lay the mushroom caps on a buttered baking tray. Spoon the filling evenly into each mushroom. Bake for 30 minutes.

KARTOFFELPUFFER (Potato Pancakes)

Preparation time: 10 minutes
Cooking time: 15 minutes

IMPERIAL (METRIC)	AMERICAN
2 lb (900g) potatoes, peeled	*2 lb potatoes, peeled*
5 oz (140g) onion, diced	*1 cupful diced onion*
1 teaspoonful sea salt	*1 teaspoonful sea salt*
3 eggs	*3 eggs*
6 oz (170g) gram flour, sifted	*1⅛ cupful chick pea flour, sifted*
Sunflower oil for frying	*Sunflower oil for frying*
Parsley to garnish	*Parsley to garnish*

1. Grate the potatoes into a bowl. Add the onion, salt and eggs and stir well. Then add the flour, stirring all the time to avoid lumps, making sure all the potato is coated.
2. Heat about ¼-inch (0.5cm) oil in a large frying pan. Use about 4 tablespoonsful of the potato mixture for each pancake; place it in the pan in a lump, then flatten it out to about 5 inches (12.5cm). (In a large enough pan, you should be able to do 3 or 4 pancakes at one time.) When the edges brown, turn the pancakes over and cook the other side.
3. Remove the pancakes from the pan with a slotted spoon and drain. Pile them on a large serving dish and keep warm in the oven. When ready to serve, garnish generously with parsley.

CREAMED CHICORY

Preparation time: 10 minutes
Baking time: 40 minutes

IMPERIAL (METRIC)
8 heads chicory
2 oz (55g) butter
Sea salt and freshly ground black
* pepper*
½ pint (300ml) single cream

AMERICAN
8 heads Belgian endive
4 tablespoonsful butter
Sea salt and freshly ground black
* pepper*
1¼ cupsful light cream

1. Trim the chicory (endive) and cut each one in half lengthways. Blanch with boiling water and leave for a few minutes. Drain well.
2. Preheat the oven to 375°F/190°C (Gas Mark 5).
3. Butter a large baking dish, place the chicory (endive) in and dot with butter. Season to taste, then bake for 30 minutes.
4. Pour the cream over the chicory (endive) and bake for another 10 minutes.

DAMSON CREAM

Preparation time: 20 minutes
Cooking time: 20 minutes

IMPERIAL (METRIC)
1½ lb (680g) damsons
3 fl oz (90ml) sweet sherry
2 tablespoonsful honey
2 eggs, separated
1 pint (600ml) double cream
Crystallized violets to decorate

AMERICAN
1½ lb damson plums
6 tablespoonsful sweet sherry
2 tablespoonsful honey
2 eggs, separated
2½ cupsful heavy cream
Crystallized violets to decorate

1. Cook the damsons with the sherry and honey until soft.
2. Put through a sieve to remove stones and skins, then purée in a blender until smooth.
3. Whisk the egg whites until stiff. Whip the cream until stiff.
4. Mix the egg yolks with the damson purée in a large bowl. Fold in the cream, then the egg whites.
5. Serve in individual glasses and decorate with crystallized violets.

AUTUMN MENU 5

Green Jade Soup	**Hot Sake or Tea**
Green Beans with Fried Bean Curd	**Dry White**
Chinese Potato Pancakes	**Chardonnay**
Sweet and Sour Beans	**or Riesling**
Deep-Fried Marrow with Dates and Bamboo Shoots	
Noodles or Boiled Rice	
Sesame Biscuits with Fruits	

GREEN JADE SOUP

(Illustrated opposite page 168.)
Cooking time: Cooking the spinach, plus 20 minutes

IMPERIAL (METRIC)	AMERICAN
2 tablespoonsful olive oil	*2 tablespoonsful olive oil*
6 oz (170g) diced onion	*1 cupful diced onion*
1 teaspoonful grated root ginger	*1 teaspoonful grated ginger root*
1 teaspoonful ground coriander	*1 teaspoonful ground coriander*
½ lb (225g) cooked, puréed spinach	*½ lb cooked, puréed spinach*
1 teaspoonful sea salt	*1 teaspoonful sea salt*
Pinch of pepper and five-spice powder	*Pinch of pepper and five-spice powder*
3 pints (1.8 litre) celery stock (see page 49)	*7½ cupsful celery stock (see page 49)*
Flaked almonds to garnish	*Slivered almonds to garnish*

1. Heat the oil in a frying pan and cook the onion, ginger and coriander until the onion is soft. Add the spinach, salt, pepper and five-spice powder. Pour in the celery stock. Mix and simmer for 15 minutes.
2. Taste and correct the seasoning.
3. Serve in a soup tureen and float almonds on the surface of the soup.

GREEN BEANS WITH FRIED BEAN CURD

(Illustrated opposite.)

Preparation time: 15 minutes
Cooking time: 15 minutes

IMPERIAL (METRIC)	AMERICAN
4 cakes bean curd	*4 cakes bean curd*
4 tablespoonsful sunflower oil	*4 tablespoonsful sunflower oil*
2 tablespoonsful soya sauce	*2 tablespoonsful soy sauce*
1 tablespoonful dry sherry	*1 tablespoonful dry sherry*
1 lb (450g) runner beans	*1 lb green beans*
1 teaspoonful arrowroot	*1 teaspoonful arrowroot*
2 tablespoonsful vegetable stock	*2 tablespoonsful vegetable stock*

1. Slice the bean curd. Heat half the oil in a wok or frying pan and fry the bean curd until it begins to turn golden or shrivel a bit at the edges. Remove from the pan. Mix the soy sauce and sherry and dip the bean curd in the mixture.
2. Top and tail the beans and cut diagonally into 1-inch (2.5cm) slices. Heat the remaining oil and stir-fry the beans for about 3 minutes.
3. Add the bean curd and marinade to the pan.
4. Dissolve the arrowroot in the stock and pour into the pan. Stir and continue to cook until the sauce thickens a little.

Opposite: Green Jade Soup (page 167) *and* Green Beans with Fried Bean Curd (above).
Overleaf: Autumn Menu 3 (pages 160 to 163).
Opposite page 169: Honey and Cognac Ice Cream (page 187).

CHINESE POTATO PANCAKES

Preparation time: 10 minutes
Cooking time: 30 minutes
Chilling time: 1 hour

IMPERIAL (METRIC)
2 lb (900g) potatoes, peeled
6 oz (170g) spring onions, chopped
4 cloves garlic, crushed
4 tablespoonsful toasted sesame seeds
2 tablespoonsful soya sauce
Gram or plain flour to dust
Sunflower oil for frying
Sea salt and freshly ground black
    pepper
Additional sesame seeds to sprinkle

AMERICAN
2 lb potatoes, peeled
1 cupful chopped scallions
4 cloves garlic, crushed
4 tablespoonsful toasted sesame seeds
2 tablespoonsful soy sauce
Chick pea or all-purpose flour to
    dust
Sunflower oil for frying
Sea salt and freshly ground black
    pepper
Additional sesame seeds to sprinkle

1. Boil potatoes until tender. Mash, then mix in the spring onion (scallion), garlic, sesame seeds and soya sauce.
2. Form the mixture into golf-sized balls, then flatten and dust with flour. Refrigerate for 1 hour.
3. Heat the sunflower oil in a frying pan and fry until golden. Drain and keep warm in the oven. Serve with sesame seeds sprinkled over.

SWEET AND SOUR BEANS

Cooking time: 10 minutes

IMPERIAL (METRIC)
1 lb (450g) broad beans (fresh or
    frozen)
4 oz (115g) spring onions, diced

AMERICAN
1 lb fava beans (fresh or frozen)
¾ cupful diced scallions

For the sauce:
2 teaspoonsful grated root ginger
5 cloves garlic, crushed
2 tablespoonsful cider vinegar
1 tablespoonful brown sugar
2 tablespoonsful honey
Sea salt and freshly ground black
    pepper
2 teaspoonsful arrowroot, dissolved
    in 4 fl oz (120ml) water

2 teaspoonsful grated ginger root
5 cloves garlic, crushed
2 tablespoonsful cider vinegar
1 tablespoonful brown sugar
2 tablespoonsful honey
Sea salt and freshly ground black
    pepper
2 teaspoonsful arrowroot, dissolved
    in ½ cupful water

1. Boil the broad (fava) beans until tender.
2. Meanwhile, put all the sauce ingredients in a pan and stir until it begins to thicken.
3. Drain the broad beans and add to the sauce. Pour into a serving dish and sprinkle with spring onion.

DEEP-FRIED MARROW WITH DATES AND BAMBOO SHOOTS

Preparation time: 10 minutes
Cooking time   10 minutes

IMPERIAL (METRIC)

1 lb (450g) marrow or pumpkin
8 oz (225g) dates
2 tablespoonsful sunflower oil
10 oz (275g) bamboo shoots
2 tablespoonsful soya sauce
3 fl oz (90ml) dry sherry
1 teaspoonful brown sugar
Sea salt and freshly ground black
   pepper

AMERICAN

1 lb squash or pumpkin
1¾ cupsful dates
2 tablespoonsful sunflower oil
2 cupsful bamboo shoots
2 tablespoonsful soy sauce
6 tablespoonsful dry sherry
1 teaspoonful brown sugar
Sea salt and freshly ground black
   pepper

1. Remove the rind of the marrow (squash) or pumpkin, deseed and cut into cubes. Cut the dates in half and stone.
2. Heat the oil in a wok or frying pan and fry the marrow for 2-3 minutes, add the bamboo shoots and dates. Continue cooking until the marrow is crisp.
3. Pour the remaining ingredients into the pan and heat briefly. Pour into a serving dish.

SESAME BISCUITS AND FRUITS

Preparation time: 15 minutes
Baking time: 15 minutes

IMPERIAL (METRIC)

4 oz (115g) gram or plain flour
1 teaspoonful salt
1 tablespoonful sesame oil
1 egg, beaten
2 tablespoonsful toasted sesame
   seeds

AMERICAN

¾ cupful chick pea flour or 1
   cupful all-purpose flour
1 teaspoonful salt
1 tablespoonful sesame oil
1 egg, beaten
2 tablespoonsful toasted sesame
   seeds

Fruits:
2½ lb (1.1kg) of whatever is in
   season: pears, apples,
   strawberries, plus lychees, melon,
   passion fruit

2½ lb of whatever is in season:
   pears, apples, strawberries, plus
   lychees, melon, passion fruit

1. Preheat the oven to 400°F/200°C (Gas Mark 6).
2. Sift the flour with the salt and rub in the oil until the dough is the texture of breadcrumbs. Mix in the egg to form a paste (you may need to add a little water). Roll out the dough to ¼-inch (0.5cm) thick on a floured board.
3. Cut out rounds with a biscuit cutter and sprinkle with sesame seeds. Bake for about 15 minutes, or until golden brown. Remove from the oven.
4. Prepare and slice the fruit. Arrange in a pyramid and serve with the biscuits.

AUTUMN MENU 6

Oeufs aux Pommes d'Amour   Sauvignon Blanc

Celery and Fennel Quiche   Gevrey-Chambertin
Potatoes with Russian Mushroom Sauce
Broccoli with Walnuts
Green Salad (See page 30)

Chèvre
Coeur d'Arras
Bleu de Bresse

Grapefruit and Blackcurrant Salad   Armagnac

OEUFS AUX POMMES D'AMOUR (Baked Tomatoes and Eggs)

Preparation time: 20 minutes
Cooking time: 10 minutes
Baking time: 10 minutes

IMPERIAL (METRIC)	AMERICAN
6-8 large tomatoes	*6-8 large tomatoes*
6 oz (170g) diced onion	*1 cupful diced onion*
3 cloves garlic, crushed	*3 cloves garlic, crushed*
Sea salt and freshly ground black pepper	*Sea salt and freshly ground black pepper*
1 tablespoonful olive oil	*1 tablespoonful olive oil*
3 fl oz (90ml) white wine	*6 tablespoonsful white wine*
6-8 egg yolks	*6-8 egg yolks*
4 oz (115g) grated parmesan cheese	*1 cupful grated parmesan cheese*
Watercress to garnish	*Watercress to garnish*

1. Cut the tops off the tomatoes and discard. Scoop out the flesh carefully, so that the shell is intact. Place the shells upside down to drain and chop the tomato flesh.
2. Add the tomato flesh to the onion, garlic and seasoning. Heat the olive oil in a pan and cook the tomato mixture. When it is soft, add the wine and reduce until it is thick. Allow to cool.
3. Preheat the oven to 425°F/220°C (Gas Mark 7). Place a little sauce inside each tomato case, then slide in 1 egg yolk and cover with the remaining sauce. Sprinkle with parmesan cheese.
4. Bake for 10 minutes and serve garnished with watercress.

CELERY AND FENNEL QUICHE
Preparation time: 10 minutes
Baking time: 25 minutes
Cooking time: 20 minutes

IMPERIAL (METRIC)	AMERICAN
8 oz (225g) shortcrust pastry	*Shortcrust pastry for an 8-inch, one-crust pie*

For the filling:

1 bunch celery	*1 bunch celery*
1 lb (450g) fennel	*1 lb fennel*
2 oz (55g) butter	*4 tablespoonsful butter*
2 bay leaves	*2 bay leaves*
1 tablespoonful water	*1 tablespoonful water*
1 oz (30g) plain flour	*¼ cupful all-purpose flour*
8 fl oz (240ml) milk	*1 cupful milk*
2 oz (55g) grated sage derby cheese	*½ cupful grated vermont sage cheese*
2 oz (55g) grated gruyère cheese	*½ cupful grated unprocessed gruyère cheese*

1. Roll out the pastry and line an 8-inch (20cm) tart tin. Bake blind in an oven preheated to 400°F/200°C (Gas Mark 6) for 20 minutes. Leave to cool.
2. Chop the celery, discarding the fibres and cut the fennel into rings. Melt half the butter in a pan. Add the celery, bay leaves and fennel and sauté lightly for 10 minutes, stirring so that the vegetables do not stick or burn. Add 1 tablespoonful water and simmer with the lid on for a further 5 minutes. Remove the bay leaves and discard.
3. Melt the remaining butter in another saucepan and add the flour to make a roux. Add the milk and grated cheeses and stir until thick and smooth. Add the juices from the vegetables and mix in.
4. Pour the vegetables into the pastry case and cover with the sauce. Place back in the oven for 5 minutes to reheat, then place beneath a hot grill to brown.

POTATOES WITH RUSSIAN MUSHROOM SAUCE
Preparation time: 15 minutes
Cooking time: 35 minutes

IMPERIAL (METRIC)	AMERICAN
3 lb (1.3kg) new potatoes	*3 lb new potatoes*
2 oz (55g) butter	*4 tablespoonsful butter*
1 lb (450g) mushrooms, sliced	*1 lb mushrooms, sliced*
1 diced onion	*1 diced onion*
1 tablespoonful flour	*1 tablespoonful flour*
½ pint (300ml) soured cream	*1¼ cupsful sour cream*
2 tablespoonsful chopped dillweed or fennel.	*2 tablespoonsful chopped dillweed or fennel*
Sea salt and freshly ground black pepper	*Sea salt and freshly ground black pepper*

1. Boil the potatoes until tender. Drain, then peel.
2. Meanwhile, prepare the sauce. Melt the butter in a saucepan and add the mushrooms and onion. Cook gently for about 10 minutes.
3. Stir in the flour and cook over a low heat, then slowly add the soured cream and dillweed or fennel. Season to taste. Remove from the heat just before the cream comes to the boil. It must not be allowed to boil.
4. Place the potatoes in a serving dish. Pour the sauce over the potatoes and serve.

BROCCOLI WITH WALNUTS

Preparation time: 10 minutes
Cooking time: 8 minutes

IMPERIAL (METRIC)	AMERICAN
2 lb (900g) broccoli	*2 lb broccoli*
2 tablespoonsful olive oil	*2 tablespoonsful olive oil*
4 oz (115g) walnuts, chopped	*1 cupful chopped walnuts*
Sea salt	*Sea salt*
2 tablespoonsful water	*2 tablespoonsful water*

1. Cut the florets from the broccoli. Discard the stalks or use them for stock.
2. Heat the oil in a saucepan, then add the walnuts and broccoli. Sprinkle with a little salt. Place over a low heat and simmer for 5 minutes.
3. Add the water and simmer for a further 2-3 minutes.
4. Serve the broccoli topped with the walnuts.

GRAPEFRUIT AND BLACKCURRANT SALAD

Preparation time: 10 minutes
Cooking time: 5 minutes
Chilling time: 1-2 hours

IMPERIAL (METRIC)	AMERICAN
6 oz (170g) blackcurrants, fresh or frozen	*1¼ cupsful blackcurrants or blackberries, fresh or frozen*
4 tablespoonsful honey	*4 tablespoonsful honey*
4 grapefruit	*4 grapefruit*

1. Cook the blackcurrants with the honey over a low heat until just soft. Leave to cool.
2. Peel the grapefruit and slice the flesh, ensuring that you have removed all the pith. (Do it over a bowl so that you can catch all the juice.)
3. Pour the blackcurrants over the grapefruit and chill before serving.

AUTUMN MENU 7

Aubergine Mousse with Beurre Blanc	Muscadet or Chablis
Tarte aux Oignons à l'Alsacienne **Cauliflower with Parsley Butter** **Potato and Mint Pilaf**	Beaujolais-Villages or Côte Rôtie
Tomme de Belleville **Roquefort**	Marc from Frontignan or Elderberry Brandy from Alsace
Crème Brûlée	

AUBERGINE MOUSSE WITH BEURRE BLANC

Preparation time: 10 minutes
Cooking time: 15 minutes
Baking time: 20 minutes

IMPERIAL (METRIC)
2 tablespoonsful olive oil
18 oz (505g) aubergine, pared and
  cut into small pieces
2 oz (55g) shallots, chopped
3 cloves garlic, crushed
2 tablespoonsful tarragon, finely
  chopped
4 eggs
¾ pint (450ml) single cream
Sea salt and freshly ground black
  pepper

AMERICAN
2 tablespoonsful olive oil
1 large eggplant, pared and diced
⅓ cupful chopped shallots
3 cloves garlic, crushed
2 tablespoonsful tarragon, finely
  chopped
4 eggs
2 cupsful light cream
Sea salt and freshly ground black
  pepper

For the sauce:
3 oz (85g) unsalted butter
3 tablespoonsful white wine vinegar
5 tablespoonsful dry white wine
1 teaspoonful chopped shallots
1 tablespoonful double cream
Sea salt and freshly ground black
  pepper

6 tablespoonsful unsalted butter
3 tablespoonsful white wine vinegar
5 tablespoonsful dry white wine
1 teaspoonful chopped shallots
1 tablespoonful heavy cream
Sea salt and freshly ground black
  pepper

1. Heat the olive oil in a saucepan and gently sauté the aubergines (eggplants), shallots, garlic and tarragon. When the aubergine is soft, remove from the heat and leave to cool.

2. Place the contents of the pan into a blender container with the eggs and purée. Add the cream, salt and pepper and blend again.
3. Preheat the oven to 450°F/220°C (Gas Mark 7).
4. Butter 6-8 ramekins with some of the butter and divide the mixture evenly amongst the ramekins. Bake for 15-20 minutes.
5. While the mousse is baking, make the sauce. Put the vinegar, wine and shallots into a saucepan and reduce until there is about 2 tablespoonsful liquid. Add the cream and when it begins to boil, lower the heat instantly and whisk in the butter.
6. To serve, pour some of the sauce into each ramekin to cover the top of the mousse.

TARTE AUX OIGNONS À L'ALSACIENNE

Cooking time: 15 minutes
Baking time: Baking the pastry, plus 35 minutes

IMPERIAL (METRIC)	AMERICAN
Filling:	
2 lb (900g) onions, chopped	*2 lb onions, chopped*
2 tablespoonsful oregano	*2 tablespoonsful oregano*
4 oz (115g) butter	*½ cupful (1 stick) butter*
3 eggs	*3 eggs*
8 fl oz (240ml) single cream	*1 cupful light cream*
Sea salt, white pepper and grated nutmeg	*Sea salt, white pepper and grated nutmeg*
9-11-inch (22.5-27.5cm) tart tin lined with shortcrust pastry	*9-11-inch tart tin lined with shortcrust pastry*

1. Cook the onions and oregano in the butter slowly over a low heat for about 15 minutes; they should be soft and transparent, but not brown.
2. Mix the eggs with the cream, add a pinch of salt, white pepper and a little freshly grated nutmeg.
3. Preheat the oven to 425°F/220°C (Gas Mark 7).
4. Add the onions to the cream mixture, stir well, then pour into the pastry case.
5. Bake the tart for 15 minutes, then reduce the heat to 350°F/180°C (Gas Mark 4) and bake for another 15 minutes. Turn off the heat but leave the tart in the oven to allow it to settle for a further 5 minutes. This tart should be eaten warm.

CAULIFLOWER WITH PARSLEY BUTTER

Preparation time: 5 minutes
Cooking time: 15 minutes

IMPERIAL (METRIC)	AMERICAN
1 large cauliflower	*1 large cauliflower*
6 oz (170g) slightly salted butter, softened	*¾ cupful slightly salted butter, softened*
1½ oz (40g) chopped parsley	*¾ cupful chopped parsley*
2 teaspoonsful lemon juice	*2 teaspoonsful lemon juice*
Freshly ground black pepper	*Freshly ground black pepper*
Chopped parsley to garnish	*Chopped parsley to garnish*

1. Separate the cauliflower florets and steam for 13 minutes, or until just soft.
2. Mix the rest of the ingredients together, working it into a paste.
3. Arrange the cooked cauliflower in a serving dish and dot with the parsley butter. Add more chopped parsley before serving.

POTATO AND MINT PILAF

Preparation time: 10 minutes
Cooking time: 35 minutes

IMPERIAL (METRIC)	AMERICAN
16 small new potatoes	*16 small new potatoes*
2 oz (55g) butter	*4 tablespoonsful butter*
6 oz (170g) patna rice	*¾ cupful patna rice*
4 tablespoonsful chopped mint	*4 tablespoonsful chopped mint*
1 pint (600ml) celery stock (see page 49)	*2½ cupsful celery stock (see page 49)*
Sea salt and freshly ground black pepper	*Sea salt and freshly ground black pepper*

1. Clean and scrape the potatoes and then cut into small cubes. Melt the butter in a large pan and add the diced potatoes and rice, stir for a couple of minutes until they have absorbed the butter. Add half the mint and then the stock so that it barely covers the rice and potatoes.
2. Simmer over a very low heat for 30 minutes. Check halfway through to see that it does not need more stock. (The rice and potatoes should absorb all the stock and be tender after half an hour.) Add the rest of the mint before serving.

CRÈME BRÛLÉE

Cooking time: 15 minutes
Chilling time: 2-3 hours

IMPERIAL (METRIC)	AMERICAN
1 pint (600ml) double cream	2½ cupsful heavy cream
3 egg yolks, beaten	3 egg yolks, beaten
4 oz (115g) caster sugar	½ cupful superfine sugar
Drop of vanilla essence	Drop of vanilla extract
4 tablespoonsful dark brown sugar	4 tablespoonsful dark brown sugar

1. Beat one-quarter of the cream, egg yolks and caster sugar together. Add the vanilla essence to the rest of the cream and bring to the boil. Quickly remove from the heat and add a little of the cream mixture to the egg mixture, then incorporate both and return to the heat, stirring all the time until the mixture thickens. Do not allow to boil as it will curdle. Leave to cool.
2. Pour into 6-8 ramekins or into one large, shallow flameproof dish and refrigerate until the custard is set.
3. Sprinkle the brown sugar over the custard and pop under a very hot grill so that the sugar caramelizes. Return to the refrigerator to set and harden.

AUTUMN MENU 8

Leek Terrine   Gamay de Chautagne

Pipérade du Pays Basque   Médoc
Buckwheat Noodles   Côtes-du-Rhône
Turnips in Lemon Sauce
Green Salad with Avocado

Camembert
Tomme de Savoie

English Treacle Tart   Kirsch or Marc

LEEK TERRINE

Preparation time: 15 minutes
Cooking time: 4 minutes
Baking time: 15 minutes

IMPERIAL (METRIC)
14 even-sized young leeks
2 oz (55g) butter
Sea salt and freshly ground black
  pepper

For the sauce:
4 fl oz (120ml) olive oil
4 tablespoonsful sherry or white wine
1 teaspoonful prepared English
  mustard
1 tablespoonful chopped shallots
1 tablespoonful chopped mint
Sea salt and freshly ground black
  pepper

AMERICAN
14 even-sized young leeks
4 tablespoonsful butter
Sea salt and freshly ground black
  pepper

½ cupful olive oil
4 tablespoonsful sherry or white wine
1 teaspoonful prepared English
  mustard
1 tablespoonful chopped shallots
1 tablespoonful chopped mint
Sea salt and freshly ground black
  pepper

1. Trim the leeks, cut in half lengthways and wash carefully. See that they are all the same size and will fit neatly into a terrine dish.
2. Heat the butter in a large pan, add the leeks and cook, covered over a moderate heat for about 4 minutes.
3. Preheat the oven to 375°F/190°C (Gas Mark 5). Butter a terrine dish. Lay the leeks in the dish so that they fit neatly. Season and cover with foil, then place a weight on top.
4. Place the terrine in a *bain marie* and bake for about 10-15 minutes. Remove from the oven and leave to cool, with the weight still in place.
5. Before serving, turn out the terrine onto a serving dish. Mix all the sauce ingredients together and whisk well. To serve, slice the terrine and coat with the sauce.

PIPÉRADE DU PAYS BASQUE

Cooking time: 40 minutes

IMPERIAL (METRIC)	AMERICAN
3 tablespoonsful olive oil	*3 tablespoonsful olive oil*
4-5 green peppers, deseeded and sliced	*4-5 green peppers, seeded and sliced*
4-5 onions, finely chopped	*4-5 onions, minced*
5 large tomatoes, peeled and chopped	*5 large tomatoes, peeled and chopped*
3 cloves garlic, crushed	*3 cloves garlic, crushed*
Sea salt and freshly ground black pepper	*Sea salt and freshly ground black pepper*
6 eggs, beaten	*6 eggs, beaten*

1. Heat the olive oil in a large pan and cook the peppers and onions over a low heat, stirring now and again until they are quite soft, about 30 minutes.
2. Add the tomatoes and garlic and increase the heat. Cook for about 5 minutes to reduce the moisture in the tomatoes, so that it becomes a coarse purée. Season with salt and pepper.
3. Whisk the eggs into the mixture, stirring and moving the contents of the pan around as for scrambled eggs. When the mixture is dry, it is done. It will only take a few minutes.

BUCKWHEAT NOODLES

Cooking time: 5 minutes

Excellent noodles made in Japan can now be bought commercially. Pour boiling water over the noodles in a large pan and leave them to absorb the water for about 5 minutes, then drain.

TURNIPS IN LEMON SAUCE

Preparation time: 5 minutes
Cooking time: 12 minutes

IMPERIAL (METRIC)	AMERICAN
1½ lb (680g) small turnips	*1½ lb small turnips*
2 oz (55g) butter	*4 tablespoonsful butter*
2 teaspoonsful Meaux mustard	*2 teaspoonsful Meaux mustard*
2 tablespoonsful lemon juice	*2 tablespoonsful lemon juice*
Sea salt and freshly ground black pepper	*Sea salt and freshly ground black pepper*

1. Trim and quarter the turnips (they do not need paring) and boil them in a little salted water for about 10 minutes, or until they are just tender. Drain well and place in a flameproof dish.
2. Melt the butter in a pan and add the mustard, lemon juice, salt and pepper. Stir well and pour over the turnips. Put the dish back on the heat and turn the turnips in the sauce so they are well-coated.

GREEN SALAD WITH AVOCADO
Preparation time: 10 minutes

IMPERIAL (METRIC)
1 ripe avocado
2 tablespoonsful sunflower oil
1 teaspoonful wine vinegar
Sea salt and freshly ground black
   pepper
1 large, crisp lettuce

AMERICAN
1 ripe avocado
2 tablespoonsful sunflower oil
1 teaspoonful wine vinegar
Sea salt and freshly ground black
   pepper
1 large, crisp lettuce

1. Cut the avocado in half and remove the stone. Scoop out the flesh and place into a blender with the oil and vinegar. Mix to a thin purée and season to taste. Pour into a large salad bowl.
2. Tear the lettuce leaves into manageable sizes and arrange in the bowl. Mix the salad just before serving by turning the lettuce in the avocado dressing.

ENGLISH TREACLE TART
Preparation time: 15 minutes
Baking time: 40 minutes

IMPERIAL (METRIC)
1 lb (450g) shortcrust pastry
1 large cooking apple, pared, cored
   and grated
2 oz (55g) fresh wholemeal
   breadcrumbs
Zest and juice of 1 lemon
Zest and juice of 1 orange
1 teaspoonful freshly grated root
   ginger
4 tablespoonsful golden syrup
2 egg yolks

AMERICAN
Shortcrust pastry for two-crust
   10-inch pie
1 large cooking apple, pared, cored
   and grated
1 cupful fresh wholewheat bread
   crumbs
Zest and juice of 1 lemon
Zest and juice of 1 orange
1 teaspoonful freshly grated root
   ginger
4 tablespoonsful golden syrup
2 egg yolks

1. Preheat the oven to 350°F/180°C (Gas Mark 4).
2. Line a 10-inch (25cm) flan tin with the pastry. Blend the remaining ingredients together, adding the egg yolks last. Pour the mixture into the pastry case. Decorate with a pastry lattice design.
3. Bake for about 40 minutes, until golden brown.

AUTUMN MENU 9

Curried Parsnip Soup	Muscadet
Croustade aux Champignons	Beaujolais-Villages
Le Pétatou	
Chou à la Paysanne	
Endive and Watercress Salad	
Chèvre Frais	
Reblochon	
Stilton	
Pommes au Beurre	Calvados

CURRIED PARSNIP SOUP

Preparation time: 10 minutes
Cooking time: 30 minutes

IMPERIAL (METRIC)
2 oz (55g) butter
1 tablespoonful olive oil
½ teaspoonful each: ground
  coriander, cumin, turmeric,
  fenugreek, cayenne pepper and
  sea salt
2 large onions, diced
3 cloves garlic, crushed
1 tablespoonful flour
3 pints (1.8 litres) celery stock (see
  page 49)
1 lb (450g) parsnips, scraped and
  sliced
½ pint (300ml) single cream
Handful of chopped parsley to
  garnish

AMERICAN
4 tablespoonsful butter
1 tablespoonful olive oil
½ teaspoonful each: ground
  coriander, cumin, turmeric,
  fenugreek, cayenne pepper and
  sea salt
2 large onions, diced
3 cloves garlic, crushed
1 tablespoonful flour
7½ cupsful celery stock (see page
  49)
1 lb parsnips, scraped and sliced
1¼ cupsful light cream
Handful of chopped parsley to
  garnish

1. Melt the butter and oil in a large saucepan and cook the spices with the onions and garlic until soft, about 10 minutes. Stir in the flour and cook for another 2 minutes.
2. Add the celery stock and parsnips. Cook until the parsnips are quite tender, about 15 minutes. Leave to cool.
3. Put the soup in a blender and blend until smooth.
4. Add the cream and reheat gently without boiling.
5. Before serving, sprinkle the parsley on top.

CROUSTADE AUX CHAMPIGNONS (Mushroom Tart)

Preparation time: 10 minutes
Chilling time: 1 hour
Baking time: 30 minutes
Cooking time: 15 minutes

IMPERIAL (METRIC)	AMERICAN
Pastry:	
4 oz (115g) butter	*½ cupful (1 stick) butter*
8 oz (225g) plain flour	*2 cupsful all-purpose flour*
Pinch of sea salt	*Pinch of sea salt*
1 large egg yolk	*1 large egg yolk*
1 tablespoonful iced water	*1 tablespoonful ice water*
Filling:	
1 lb (450g) mushrooms	*1 lb mushrooms*
5 oz (140g) butter	*⅔ cupful butter*
Juice of 1 lemon	*Juice of 1 lemon*
Sea salt and freshly ground black pepper	*Sea salt and freshly ground black pepper*
1 teaspoonful flour	*1 teaspoonful flour*
¼ pint (150ml) celery stock (see page 49)	*⅔ cupful celery stock (see page 49)*
2 egg yolks	*2 egg yolks*
2 tablespoonsful double cream	*2 tablespoonsful heavy cream*

1. First make the pastry. Cream the butter in a bowl with a wooden spoon. Sift the flour into a large mixing bowl and add a pinch of salt. Make a well in the centre and drop in the butter, egg yolk and water. Mix with a wooden spoon.
2. Gather the dough into a soft ball (you may need a little more water), wrap in cling film or greaseproof paper and refrigerate for 1 hour at least.
3. Take the dough out of the refrigerator 10 minutes before you need it. Preheat the oven to 400°F/200°C (Gas Mark 6).
4. Roll out the pastry and fit into a buttered 10-inch (25cm) flan tin. Prick the bottom with a fork and line with dried beans. Bake for 15 minutes. Reduce the heat to 375°F/190°C (Gas Mark 5) and bake for an additional 15 minutes. Watch that it does not colour too deeply (it should be light golden). If it starts to get brown, cover with foil.
5. Slice the mushrooms. Melt nearly all of the butter and cook the mushrooms in a pan with the lemon juice and a little salt and pepper, about 10 minutes.
6. In another pan, melt the remaining butter and work in the flour. Let it cook for a moment, then add the stock and the cooking liquor from the mushrooms.
7. Mix the egg yolks with the cream. Add some of the hot stock and stir, then pour back into the pan, so that the cream and egg is amalgamated with the stock. Heat gently; do not allow it to boil. When it is thickening, pour in the mushrooms.
8. Keep the pastry case warm in the oven. Pour in the mushroom mixture and serve.

LE PÉTATOU (Soufflé Potatoes with Curd Cheese)

Preparation time: 10 minutes
Cooking time: 20 minutes
Baking time: 20 minutes

IMPERIAL (METRIC)	AMERICAN
1 lb (450g) potatoes, peeled	*1 lb potatoes, peeled*
2 oz (55g) butter	*4 tablespoonsful butter*
4 oz (115g) curd cheese	*½ cupful curd cheese*
2 large eggs, separated	*2 large eggs, separated*
Sea salt and white pepper	*Sea salt and white pepper*

1. Boil the potatoes until tender. Drain well.
2. Preheat the oven to 400°F/200°C (Gas Mark 6).
3. Mash the potatoes, adding the butter and curd cheese to make a smooth purée. Beat in the egg yolks. Season to taste. Whisk the egg whites until stiff and fold into the potato mixture.
4. Pour the mixture into a buttered ovenproof dish and bake until the potato has risen and is golden brown, about 20 minutes. Serve at once.

CHOU À LA PAYSANNE (Cabbage with Leeks and Onions)

Preparation time: 15 minutes
Cooking time: 15 minutes

IMPERIAL (METRIC)	AMERICAN
2 large onions	*2 large onions*
2 large leeks	*2 large leeks*
1 large, firm cabbage	*1 large, firm cabbage*
1 oz (30g) butter	*2 tablespoonsful butter*
Sea salt and freshly ground black pepper	*Sea salt and freshly ground black pepper*
Handful of fresh chopped mint	*Handful of fresh chopped mint*

1. Coarsely chop the onions. Slice the leeks lengthways and clean, then cut into 1-inch (2.5cm) slices. Quarter the cabbage and cut away the core, then cut each quarter into ½-inch (1.25cm) slices.
2. Melt the butter in a heavy cast iron casserole and put the chopped onions on the bottom. Season well with salt and pepper. Lay in the cabbage and season lightly. Fit the leeks into the chinks so that all the vegetables are tightly wedged together. Fit a piece of greaseproof paper over the top and place the lid on the casserole.
3. Place the casserole over a low heat until it begins to bubble, then lower the heat to the minimum and cook for about 10 minutes. The cabbage should still be *al dente*. Test and if it needs a little more time, give it 5 minutes, but no longer.
4. Scatter the mint over the top before serving.

POMMES AU BEURRE (Caramel Apple Slices)

Preparation time: 10 minutes
Cooking time: 15 minutes

IMPERIAL (METRIC)
Juice of 1 lemon
1½ lb (680g) Cox's apples
2 oz (55g) unsalted butter
Raw cane sugar

AMERICAN
Juice of 1 lemon
1½ lb McIntosh apples
4 tablespoonsful unsalted butter
Raw cane sugar

1. Pour the lemon juice into a soup plate. Pare and core the apples, cut into rings about ½-inch (1.25cm) thick and dip them in the lemon juice, turning them to coat all surfaces.
2. Melt the butter in a frying pan and coat both sides of the apple rings with the butter. Arrange a single layer of apples in a large flat pan and cook until the apples are browned underneath. Heat the grill.
3. Place the pan of apples under the grill and cook for another 2 minutes, so that the tops are browned. Sprinkle with the sugar and continue to grill until the sugar caramelizes.
4. Allow to cool a little before serving so that the sugar hardens and crisps.

AUTUMN MENU 10

Celeri Sicilienne	Chardonnay
Baked Avocado with Onion Sauce	Corbières de
Gratin of Beetroot	Roussillon
Savoury Rice	
Green Salad (See page 30)	
Fourme d'Ambert	
Mature Cheddar	
Honey and Cognac Ice Cream	Marc

CELERI SICILIENNE (Sicilian Celeriac Salad)

Preparation time: 10 minutes

IMPERIAL (METRIC)	AMERICAN
2 celeriac roots	*2 celeriac roots*
3 tablespoonsful olive oil	*3 tablespoonsful olive oil*
2 cloves garlic, crushed	*2 cloves garlic, crushed*
2 teaspoonsful lemon juice	*2 teaspoonsful lemon juice*
Pinch of celery salt	*Pinch of celery salt*
Sea salt and freshly ground black pepper	*Sea salt and freshly ground black pepper*
2 russet apples, unpared	*2 russet apples, unpared*
6 tomatoes, sliced	*6 tomatoes, sliced*
2 14-oz (395g) tins artichoke bottoms, sliced	*2 14-oz cans artichoke bottoms, sliced*
Lettuce leaves and black olives to garnish	*Lettuce leaves and black olives to garnish*

1. Pare and grate the celeriac. Blanch in boiling water for 2 minutes. Drain.
2. Combine the olive oil, garlic, lemon juice, celery and sea salts and pepper and whisk together.
3. Grate the apples (including peel) and mix into the dressing. Add the well-drained celeriac, tomatoes and artichoke bottoms. Toss in a large bowl.
4. To serve, arrange lettuce leaves on a large platter and pile the celeriac mixture in the centre. Garnish with a few stoned black olives.

BAKED AVOCADO WITH ONION SAUCE

Preparation time: 15 minutes
Cooking time: 10 minutes
Baking time: 15 minutes

IMPERIAL (METRIC)	AMERICAN
3-4 ripe avocados	*3-4 ripe avocados*
Juice of 1 lemon	*Juice of 1 lemon*
2 large onions, diced	*2 large onions, diced*
2 oz (55g) butter	*4 tablespoonsful butter*
1 oz (30g) flour	*¼ cupful flour*
Sea salt, freshly ground black pepper, and a pinch of nutmeg	*Sea salt, freshly ground black pepper, and a pinch of nutmeg*
6 fl oz (180ml) milk	*¾ cupful milk*
1 tablespoonful capers	*1 tablespoonful capers*
1 tablespoonful green peppercorns	*1 tablespoonful green peppercorns*
Wholemeal breadcrumbs	*Wholewheat bread crumbs*

1. Cut avocados in half and remove the stones. Scoop out some of the avocado flesh and cut into cubes, leaving a ¼-inch (.5cm) shell. Sprinkle the cut surfaces of the shell and the scooped-out flesh with lemon juice and set aside.
2. Cook the onion in the butter until soft, add the flour, salt, pepper and nutmeg and cook for an additional 2-3 minutes. Add the milk to make a sauce, then add the capers, green peppercorns and avocado flesh. Remove from the heat and let cool a little.
3. Preheat the oven to 400°F/200°C (Gas Mark 6). Fill the avocado shells with the sauce, sprinkle with the breadcrumbs and bake for 15 minutes.

GRATIN OF BEETROOT

Preparation time: 10 minutes
Baking time: 15 minutes

IMPERIAL (METRIC)	AMERICAN
4-6 large cooked beetroot, skinned	*4-6 large cooked beets, skinned*
2 tablespoonsful grated parmesan cheese	*2 tablespoonsful grated parmesan cheese*
3 tablespoonsful grated cheddar cheese	*3 tablespoonsful grated cheddar cheese*
Sea salt and freshly ground black pepper	*Sea salt and freshly ground black pepper*
¼ pint (150ml) single cream	*⅔ cupful light cream*

1. Chop the beetroot. Preheat the oven to 400°F/200°C (Gas Mark 6).
2. Butter a gratin dish and sprinkle some of the cheese on the bottom. Place half of the beetroot in the dish, add more cheese, then the remaining beetroot, the rest of the cheese and the seasoning. Pour in the cream and bake for 15 minutes.

SAVOURY RICE

Preparation time: 10 minutes
Cooking time: 25 minutes

IMPERIAL (METRIC)	AMERICAN
2 onions, diced	*2 onions, diced*
3 cloves garlic, crushed	*3 cloves garlic, crushed*
1 teaspoonful grated root ginger	*1 teaspoonful grated root ginger*
1 teaspoonful each: ground coriander, cumin, fennel, fenugreek and poppy seeds	*1 teaspoonful each: ground coriander, cumin, fennel, fenugreek and poppy seeds*
2 tablespoonsful olive oil	*2 tablespoonsful olive oil*
1 lb (450g) patna rice	*2 cupsful patna rice*
Sea salt	*Sea salt*
1 tablespoonful each: sultanas and raisins	*1 tablespoonful each: golden seedless raisins and raisins*
1½ tablespoonsful each: chopped walnuts and almonds	*1½ tablespoonsful each: chopped walnuts and almonds*
1 tablespoonful paprika	*1 tablespoonful paprika*
1 tablespoonful garam masala	*1 tablespoonful garam masala*

1. Cook the onion, garlic, ginger and spices in the olive oil until the onion is soft.
2. Boil the rice in salted water until just done. Leave to rest, then drain well. Add the onion mixture, dried fruit and nuts. Keep in a warm oven to dry out for another 5 minutes.
3. Just before serving, stir in the paprika and garam masala.

HONEY AND COGNAC ICE CREAM

(Illustrated opposite page 169.)
Preparation time: 15 minutes
Freezing time: 2-3 hours

IMPERIAL (METRIC)	AMERICAN
6 eggs, separated	*6 eggs, separated*
½ lb (225g) icing sugar	*1¾ cupsful confectioner's sugar*
½ lb (225g) clear honey	*¾ cupful clear honey*
¼ pint (150ml) cognac or brandy	*⅔ cupful cognac or brandy*
¾ pint (450ml) double cream	*2 cupsful heavy cream*
Langue de chat biscuits to serve	*Langue de chat biscuits or vanilla wafers to serve*

1. Whisk the egg whites until stiff. Add the icing sugar and whisk again until very stiff and glossy.
2. Combine the beaten egg yolks with the honey and brandy in a second bowl. Add to the whisked egg whites and blend together.
3. Whip the cream until stiff and blend into the egg mixture. Freeze for 2-3 hours.
4. Serve in individual glasses accompanied by the biscuits.

AUTUMN MENU 11

Insalata di Fontina	Verdicchio or Frascati
Mushroom Pie Fèves à la Tourangelle Potato Cakes	Cabernet di Pramaggiore
Vacherin Mont-d'Or Igny Olivet Bleu	
Salade de Fruits à la Crème Brûlée	Muscat de Beaumes- de-Venise

INSALATA DI FONTINA (Cheese and Pepper Salad)

Preparation time: 15 minutes

IMPERIAL (METRIC)	AMERICAN
4 large yellow peppers	*4 large yellow peppers*
2 tablespoonsful olive oil	*2 tablespoonsful olive oil*
1 tablespoonful Dijon mustard	*1 tablespoonful Dijon mustard*
1 teaspoonful wine vinegar	*1 teaspoonful wine vinegar*
Sea salt and freshly ground black * pepper*	*Sea salt and freshly ground black* * pepper*
2 tablespoonsful double cream	*2 tablespoonsful heavy cream*
½ lb (225g) fontina cheese, diced	*½ lb fontina cheese, diced*
12 green olives, stoned and chopped	*12 green olives, pitted and chopped*

1. Grill the peppers so that the outer skins blister. Cool slightly, then peel. Deseed and slice into strips.
2. Mix the oil, mustard, vinegar, salt, pepper and cream together.
3. Mix the peppers, cheese and olives with the dressing in a salad bowl and serve.

Note: If fontina cheese is unavailable, substitute gruyère or emmental.

MUSHROOM PIE

Preparation time: 20 minutes
Chilling time: 1-2 hours
Cooking time: 5 minutes
Baking time: 35 minutes

IMPERIAL (METRIC)	AMERICAN
Cheese Pastry:	
4 oz (115g) wholemeal flour	*1 cupful wholewheat flour*
4 oz (115g) plain flour	*1 cupful all-purpose flour*
Sea salt and freshly ground black pepper	*Sea salt and freshly ground black pepper*
6 oz (170g) butter, chilled	*¾ cupful butter, chilled*
2 oz (55g) mature cheddar cheese, grated	*½ cupful grated aged cheddar cheese*
2-3 tablespoonsful water	*2-3 tablespoonsful water*
Filling:	
4 oz (115g) butter	*½ cupful (1 stick) butter*
1 lb (450g) mushrooms, sliced	*1 lb mushrooms, sliced*
2 large onions, chopped	*2 large onions, chopped*
Sea salt and freshly ground black pepper	*Sea salt and freshly ground black pepper*
1 tablespoonful chopped sage	*1 tablespoonful chopped sage*
6 oz (170g) patna rice, cooked	*¾ cupful patna rice, cooked*
3-4 hard-boiled eggs, halved	*3-4 hard-cooked eggs, halved*

1. Make the pastry. Sift the flour with the salt and pepper. Take the butter directly from the refrigerator and grate into the flour. Add the cheese and water and mix to a paste. Gather the dough up into a ball, wrap in cling film or greaseproof paper and refrigerate for 1-2 hours.
2. When ready to assemble the pie, preheat the oven to 425°F/220°C (Gas Mark 7).
3. Butter the bottom and sides of a 10-inch (25cm) pie dish with half the butter. Sauté the mushrooms in the remaining butter. Arrange the mushrooms and onions in the bottom of the pie dish, season and sprinkle with sage. Add the rice, then the eggs.
4. Roll out the pastry and fit over the top.
5. Bake for 30-35 minutes, protecting the pastry with a piece of greaseproof paper.

FÈVES À LA TOURANGELLE
Cooking time: 20 minutes

IMPERIAL (METRIC)	AMERICAN
2 lb (900g) frozen broad beans	*2 lb frozen fava beans*
1 bunch spring onions, sliced	*1 bunch scallions, sliced*
2 oz (55g) butter	*4 tablespoonsful butter*
2 tablespoonsful chopped tarragon	*2 tablespoonsful chopped tarragon*
Sea salt and freshly ground black pepper	*Sea salt and freshly ground black pepper*
2 tablespoonsful double cream	*2 tablespoonsful heavy cream*
1 egg yolk	*1 egg yolk*
2 tablespoonsful chopped parsley	*2 tablespoonsful chopped parsley*

1.   Boil the beans until they are tender. Drain.
2.   Cook the spring onions in the butter with the tarragon. When the onions are soft, add them to the beans. Season with salt and pepper. Add the cream, then the egg yolk, stirring well. Just when the sauce begins to thicken, remove the pan from the heat and pour the contents into a serving dish. Sprinkle with chopped parsley.

POTATO CAKES
Preparation time: 15 minutes
Cooking time: 35 minutes

IMPERIAL (METRIC)	AMERICAN
1 lb (450g) potatoes	*1 lb potatoes*
Sea salt and freshly ground black pepper	*Sea salt and freshly ground black pepper*
4 oz (115g) butter	*½ cupful (1 stick) butter*
4 oz (115g) plain or gram flour	*1 cupful all-purpose or chick pea flour*
Sunflower oil for frying	*Sunflower oil for frying*

1.   Boil the potatoes until tender. Peel, mash, sieve and season with salt and pepper. Add the butter to the potatoes in a bowl while the potatoes are still warm and gradually add the sifted flour until you have a firm dough.
2.   Fashion the dough into a large ball, then roll it out into a long sausage shape, making it uniform in thickness. Cut into ½-inch (1.25cm) slices.
3.   Heat a little oil in a frying pan. When it is very hot, quickly brown the potato cakes. Drain and keep warm in the oven.

SALADE DE FRUITS À LA CRÈME BRÛLÉE

Preparation time: 20 minutes
Grilling time: 5 minutes
Chilling time: 1 hour

IMPERIAL (METRIC)	AMERICAN
A combination of pears, apples, oranges, pink grapefruit, mangoes, grapes, strawberries, pineapple, plums and nectarines (about 1½-2 lb/680-900g total)	*A combination of pears, apples, oranges, pink grapefruit, mangoes, grapes, strawberries, pineapple, plums and nectarines (about 1½-2 lb total)*
4 tablespoonsful kirsch	*4 tablespoonsful kirsch*
½ pint (300ml) double cream	*1¼ cupsful double cream*
Raw cane sugar	*Raw cane sugar*

1. Prepare the fruit (pare, peel, slice, etc.) and arrange in a shallow ovenproof dish. Sprinkle with the kirsch.
2. Spread the cream on top of the fruit, then sprinkle enough sugar on so that no cream is visible.
3. Place the dish beneath a very hot grill so that the sugar melts, making sure the cream does not. Pop the dish into the refrigerator for the sugar to harden.

AUTUMN MENU 12

Les Oeufs Vert Galant   Bâtard-Montrachet

Gnocchi di Patate   Fleurie
Spiced Red Cabbage
Runner Beans (See page 158)
Lettuce Hearts with Cream Dressing

Vacherin des Bauges
Magnum
Stilton

Mango Mousse   Calvados

LES OEUFS VERT GALANT (Egg and Sweetcorn Tartlets)

Preparation time: Preparing the tartlets and cooking the eggs, plus 5 minutes
Baking time: 10 minutes

IMPERIAL (METRIC)   AMERICAN
6-8 3-inch (7.5cm) tartlet cases   *6-8 3-inch tartlet cases*
9 oz (255g) cooked sweetcorn   *1½ cupsful cooked corn*
6-8 poached eggs or oeufs mollets   *6-8 poached eggs or oeufs mollets*
3 tablespoonsful green peppercorns   *3 tablespoonsful green peppercorns*
3 tablespoonsful double cream   *3 tablespoonsful heavy cream*
Sea salt   *Sea salt*

1. Preheat the oven to 350°F/180°C (Gas Mark 4).
2. Place the tartlet cases on a baking tray and place in the oven to warm through. Remove from the oven, but do not turn the oven off.
3. Heat the sweetcorn and place a tablespoonful or two in the bottom of each tartlet.
4. Lay a poached egg or *oeuf mollet* on the sweetcorn.
5. Mix the peppercorns and cream together and season with a little salt. Spoon some over each egg.
6. Place the filled tartlets in the oven for 4-5 minutes to heat through. Serve warm.

Note: Oeufs mollets are eggs boiled so that the white has just firmed, but the yolk is still liquid (see page 141). If poaching the eggs, they should only be lightly poached.

GNOCCHI DI PATATE (Potato Gnocchi)

Preparation time: Making tomato sauce, plus 15 minutes
Chilling time: 1 hour
Cooking time: 15 minutes

IMPERIAL (METRIC)
2 lb (900g) boiled potatoes, peeled
8 oz (225g) plain or gram flour
1 teaspoonful baking powder
2 eggs, beaten
Sea salt and freshly ground black
*   pepper*
2 oz (55g) butter, melted
3 tablespoonful freshly grated
*   parmesan cheese*
Tomato sauce to serve (see page 84)

AMERICAN
2 lb boiled potatoes, peeled
2 cupsful all-purpose or chick pea
*   flour*
1 teaspoonful baking powder
2 eggs, beaten
Sea salt and freshly ground black
*   pepper*
4 tablespoonsful butter, melted
3 tablespoonsful freshly grated
*   parmesan cheese*
Tomato sauce to serve (see page 84)

1. Sieve the boiled potatoes to make a dry purée. Sift the flour and baking powder together, mix into the potatoes and add the eggs, salt and pepper. Spread out on a dish and chill for 1 hour.
2. Roll the dough into long, thin sausages, about the thickness of a finger. Cut into 1-inch (2.5cm) lengths. Bend into crescents.
3. Bring a large saucepan full of salted water to the boil, let it simmer steadily (not too violently, since that will break the gnocchi), and drop in 4 or 5 gnocchi at a time. In about 4 minutes they will pop up to the surface; take them out with a slotted spoon and keep warm by pouring a little of the melted butter into an ovenproof dish and placing the cooked gnocchi in and setting the dish in a warm oven.
4. When all the gnocchi have been cooked, pour the rest of the butter over them and sprinkle the grated parmesan cheese over the top. Keep in the oven long enough to melt the cheese, about 5 minutes.
5. Serve with the tomato sauce, brought to the table in a sauceboat, for the guests to help themselves.

SPICED RED CABBAGE

Preparation time:　15 minutes
Baking time:　2½-3 hours

IMPERIAL (METRIC)	AMERICAN
2 tablespoonsful olive oil	2 tablespoonsful olive oil
3 cloves garlic, crushed	3 cloves garlic, crushed
1 teaspoonful ground cinnamon	1 teaspoonful ground cinnamon
1 teaspoonful allspice	1 teaspoonful allspice
1 large red cabbage, thinly sliced	1 large red cabbage, thinly sliced
3 large cooking apples, pared, cored and cubed	3 large cooking apples, pared, cored and cubed
4 tablespoonsful wine or cider vinegar	4 tablespoonsful wine or cider vinegar
Sea salt and freshly ground black pepper	Sea salt and freshly ground black pepper

1. Heat the oil in a large cast iron casserole with a close-fitting lid. Stir in the garlic, cinnamon and allspice, cook for a minute, then add the cabbage, turning it over in the oil. Layer the apples on top.
2. Preheat the oven to 350°F/180°C (Gas Mark 4).
3. Pour the vinegar into the casserole, season and increase the heat so that it steams. Cover the casserole and bake for 2½-3 hours.

LETTUCE HEARTS WITH CREAM DRESSING

Preparation time:　10 minutes

IMPERIAL (METRIC)	AMERICAN
4 lettuce hearts	4 lettuce hearts
½ pint (300ml) double cream	1¼ cupsful heavy cream
6 tablespoonsful olive oil	6 tablespoonsful olive oil
2 tablespoonsful wine vinegar	2 tablespoonsful wine vinegar
Sea salt	Sea salt
2 teaspoonsful paprika	2 teaspoonsful paprika
2 tablespoonsful chopped parsley	2 tablespoonsful chopped parsley
1 tablespoonful flaked almonds	1 tablespoonful slivered almonds

1. Cut the lettuce hearts into quarters and place in a salad bowl.
2. Whisk the cream with the oil, vinegar, salt and paprika.
3. Pour the dressing over the lettuce and garnish with the parsley and almonds.

MANGO MOUSSE

Preparation time:	20 minutes
Cooking time:	10 minutes
Chilling time:	2 hours

IMPERIAL (METRIC)	AMERICAN
Purée:	
3 ripe mangoes	*3 ripe mangoes*
Juice of 1 lemon	*Juice of 1 lemon*
1 oz (30g) agar-agar	*4 tablespoonsful agar-agar*
Sabayon:	
6 egg yolks	*6 egg yolks*
4 oz (115g) icing sugar	*1 cupful confectioner's sugar*
4 fl oz (120ml) double cream, whipped	*½ cupful heavy cream, whipped*
Meringue:	
6 egg whites	*6 egg whites*
3 oz (85g) caster sugar	*6 tablespoonsful superfine sugar*
Juice of 1 lemon	*Juice of 1 lemon*

1. Peel and stone the mangoes, put the flesh in a blender container and liquidize. Heat the lemon juice, melt the agar-agar in it, add to the mango and mix well.
2. Make the sabayon. Whisk the egg yolks and sugar in a bowl over hot water until warm. Remove from the heat and continue to whisk until cold. Mix the mango purée into the sabayon, then fold in the cream.
3. Make the meringue. Whisk the egg whites until stiff. Add the sugar and lemon juice and continue to whisk until glossy. Fold into the mango purée. Place into moulds and chill well before serving, about 2 hours. To serve, unmould onto individual plates.

Note: Agar-agar can be bought in health food shops, delicatessens, Oriental food shops and large department stores.

AUTUMN MENU 13

Stuffed Pepper Salad	Chablis Grand Cru
Welsh Pie	Margaux
Haricot Bean Purée	
Brussels Sprouts with Chestnuts	
Chambarand	
Cantal	
Camembert	
	Muscat de
	Beaumes-de-Venise
Elizabeth Moxon's Lemon Posset	

STUFFED PEPPER SALAD

Preparation time: 20 minutes
Chilling time: 1 hour

IMPERIAL (METRIC)	AMERICAN
2 red peppers	*2 red peppers*
2 green peppers	*2 green peppers*
½ lb (225g) fromage frais or *Quark*	*½ lb fromage frais* or *low-fat cheese*
4 spring onions, chopped	*4 scallions, chopped*
2 tablespoonsful chopped chives	*2 tablespoonsful chopped chives*
2 tablespoonsful chopped parsley	*2 tablespoonsful chopped parsley*
2 oz (55g) butter, softened	*4 tablespoonsful butter, softened*
1 tablespoonful green peppercorns	*1 tablespoonful green peppercorns*
Sea salt and freshly ground black pepper	*Sea salt and freshly ground black pepper*
Watercress to garnish	*Watercress to garnish*

1. Cut off the tops of the peppers and scoop out the seeds and pith.
2. Beat the rest of the ingredients together.
3. Fill the peppers with the mixture, pressing down firmly. Chill for 1 hour.
4. To serve, slice the peppers into rings and arrange on a platter, garnished with watercress.

WELSH PIE

Preparation time: 15 minutes
Cooking time: 5 minutes
Baking time: 35 minutes

IMPERIAL (METRIC)
¾ lb (340g) shortcrust pastry
1 lb (450g) leeks
2 oz (55g) butter
6-8 eggs
Sea salt and freshly ground black
*   pepper*
2 tablespoonsful milk

AMERICAN
Shortcrust pastry for an 8-9-inch
*   two-crust pie*
1 lb leeks
4 tablespoonsful butter
6-8 eggs
Sea salt and freshly ground black
*   pepper*
2 tablespoonsful milk

1. Roll out half the pastry and line an 8-9-inch (20-22.5cm) pie dish. Trim the leeks and cut them in half lengthways. Melt half the butter in a pan over a very low heat, add the leeks and cook for about 5 minutes. Drain.
2. Arrange the leeks in the pie dish. Make 6-8 indentations and break in the eggs. Season and pour over the milk. Dot with the remaining butter.
3. Preheat the oven to 400°F/200°C (Gas Mark 6). Roll out the remaining pastry for a lid and place on the pie, sealing well.
4. Bake for 35 minutes or until the pastry is golden.

HARICOT BEAN PURÉE
    Preparation time: Soaking the beans overnight, plus 5 minutes
    Cooking time: 1½ hours, plus 10 minutes reheating

IMPERIAL (METRIC)
½ lb (225g) haricot beans, soaked
    overnight
3 pints (1.8 litres) vegetable stock
Juice of 2 lemons
2 cloves garlic, crushed
1 teaspoonful ground caraway seeds
2 tablespoonsful olive oil
Sea salt and freshly ground black
    pepper

AMERICAN
1 cupful navy beans, soaked
    overnight
7½ cupsful vegetable stock
Juice of 2 lemons
2 cloves garlic, crushed
1 teaspoonful ground caraway seeds
2 tablespoonsful olive oil
Sea salt and freshly ground black
    pepper

1. Boil the beans in the vegetable stock for 1½ hours. Drain any remaining liquid.
2. Preheat the oven to 350°F/180°C (Gas Mark 4).
3. Place the beans in a blender container with the lemon juice, garlic, caraway seeds, olive oil, salt and pepper. Blend to a purée.
4. Pour into an ovenproof dish and place in the oven for about 10 minutes to reheat.

BRUSSELS SPROUTS WITH CHESTNUTS
    Soaking time: Overnight
    Cooking time: 70 minutes

IMPERIAL (METRIC)
8 oz (225g) dried chestnuts, soaked
    overnight
Vegetable stock
2 lb (900g) Brussels sprouts
2 oz (55g) butter
Sea salt and freshly ground black
    pepper

AMERICAN
1⅓ cupsful dried chestnuts, soaked
    overnight
Vegetable stock
2 lb Brussels sprouts
4 tablespoonsful butter
Sea salt and freshly ground black
    pepper

1. Boil the chestnuts in enough vegetable stock to cover them for 1 hour, or until they are tender. Drain and break up into rough chunks.
2. Boil the Brussels sprouts in water until just tender, about 5-6 minutes, depending on the size of the sprouts. (Tiny ones will cook in 3 minutes.) Drain well.
3. Add the butter to the sprouts and stir in the chestnuts. Season and pour into a serving dish.

ELIZABETH MOXON'S LEMON POSSET

Preparation time: 15 minutes
Chilling time: 2 hours

IMPERIAL (METRIC)
1 pint (600ml) double cream
Finely grated zest and juice of 2
*   lemons*
¼ pint (150ml) dry white wine
1 tablespoonful caster sugar
3 egg whites
Fresh raspberries to garnish

AMERICAN
2½ cupsful heavy cream
Finely grated zest and juice of 2
*   lemons*
⅔ cupful dry white wine
1 tablespoonful superfine sugar
3 egg whites
Fresh raspberries to garnish

1. Add the lemon zest to the cream and whip until stiff. Stir in the wine and whisk in the lemon juice little by little. Add a little sugar to taste.
2. Whisk egg whites until stiff and fold into the cream mixture. Chill for 2 hours. Pour into individual glasses and garnish with fresh raspberries before serving.

INDEX OF RECIPES

INDEX OF WINES AND LIQUEURS

INDEX OF CHEESES